JEAN PAUL FRIEDRICH RICHTER

by Dorothea Berger

The purpose of this study is to reintroduce Jean Paul to the American reader who, a century ago, in his "sentimental years," was convinced that Jean Paul's works furnished enrichment both esthetically and ethically. Karl Follen and Frederick Henry Hedge at Harvard University and Henry Wadsworth Longfellow at Smith College all inspired their students to study this prolific and highly difficult German. About one hundred articles on Jean Paul were published in the United States, one third of which originated in New England; the rest emanating from New York, Philadelphia, Ohio and the South. The best English translator, Charles Timothy Brooks, was one of Follen's students. All of the Jean Paul scholars in America seemed convinced that the rewards justified the effort required to read it, whether one gained satisfaction from the pure intellectual exercise of coping with the "Colossus" or simply took pleasure in the beauties of his prose.

Jean Paul's novels were best-sellers when they were published, and his name is still well known, but his books are hardly ever read except by a small group of fervent admirers and scholars. The author of this study shows how Jean Paul, the mannerist, whom Goethe considered a "Western Oriental," is rightly claimed a forerunner and model by the more recent literary schools of Symbolism, Expressionism and Surrealism. As a poet he transforms regular life into an artistic vision and shows us symbolic meaning in our experiences.

TWAYNE'S WORLD AUTHORS SERIES (TWAS)

The purpose of TWAS is to survey the major writers —novelists, dramatists, historians, poets, philosophers, and critics—of the nations of the world. Among the national literatures covered are those of Australia, Canada, China, Eastern Europe, France, Germany, Greece, India, Italy, Japan, Latin America, the Netherlands, New Zealand, Poland, Russia, Scandinavia, Spain, and the African nations, as well as Hebrew, Yiddish, and Latin Classical literatures. This survey is complemented by Twayne's United States Authors Series and English Authors Series

The intent of each volume in these series is to present a critical-analytical study of the works of the writer; to include biographical and historical material that may be necessary for understanding, appreciation, and critical appraisal of the writer; and to present all material in clear, concise English—but not to vitiate the scholarly content of the work by doing so.

Jean Paul Friedrich Richter

By DOROTHEA BERGER

New York University

Twayne Publishers, Inc.   ::   New York

Preface

Jean Paul lives in the anonymity of his fame, i.e., his name is well known in Germany but his works are hardly read. His books were best sellers when they were published; and there has always been a group of fervent admirers and scholars enjoying his works and interpreting them—the Nestor of the group being Eduard Berend, the editor of the historical-critical edition and author of numerous articles on Jean Paul. But the average educated German knows Jean Paul only from the reports of others.[1] There seem to be two reasons for this neglect, one of them being Jean Paul's style. According to Ernst Robert Curtius's definition of mannerism (as opposed to classicism) Jean Paul would be a formal mannerist. Curtius describes the formal classicist as an author who writes "correctly, clearly and in accordance with the rules."[2] A mannerist, on the other hand, wants to say things "not normally but abnormally. . . . He wants to surprise, to astonish, to dazzle" (p. 282). Mannerism encompasses all "literary tendencies which are opposed to classicism" (p. 274), and Curtius sees in it "the complementary phenomenon of the classicism of all periods" (p. 273). Perhaps this is one of the reasons why Goethe considered Jean Paul a "Western Oriental"[3] and why the more recent literary schools of Symbolism, Expressionism, and Surrealism claimed him as one of their forerunners and models. But even this closeness to modern literary modes does not encourage contemporary readers to study his works.

The other reason for the decline of Jean Paul's fame is his attitude towards life and beauty. People of the twentieth century are embarrassed by his overwhelming enthusiasm and his passionate excesses of emotion, be it happiness, grief, friendship, love, or despair—in part, perhaps, because our generation has experienced "the bitter time when humanity was found in no hearts but in those of dogs."[4] We seem closer to those "anchorites in the desert of reason oppressed by the secret powers of mechanism."[5] Only the reader free of fear and egotism, and capable of following Jean Paul's flights of the emotions, can reach up to the beauty, the music, the raptures, "the dissolutions into dream-like calm . . . the blissful anticipation of passing away . . ." of Jean Paul's prose.[6]

Jean Paul himself divided his fictional writings into three categories: Italian novels, German novels, and Dutch novels. He borrowed these designations from the corresponding schools of painting. In his *Introduction of Esthetics*, §§72 and 73, he defines the Italian novel as that which presents idyllic scenery, noble feelings, sublime passions, and heroic characters, such as is true of Goethe's *Werther*, Rousseau's *Nouvelle Héloïse*, Wieland's *Agathon*, and his own *Titan*. The German novel is best defined by juxtaposition with the Dutch novel, which is short, sparse, and moralistic, describing the ordinary life of simple people, and suffering neither from heroic passions nor from tragic conflicts but gaining happiness through resignation. The protagonist of the Dutch novel is not idealized but is presented rather as a humorous figure. The German novel, finally, is neither sublime nor comical but allows a richly textured presentation of the everyday life of middle-class people, as exemplified by Fielding and Sterne in England and by Jean Paul's *Siebenkäs* and *Walt and Vult; or The Twins*.

Our discussion will begin with two of Jean Paul's Dutch works in the order of their creation. These two shorter narratives allow relatively easy access to his work because of their charm and humor. As an example of Jean Paul's Italian style we shall discuss two early novels, *The Invisible Lodge* and *Hesperus*, and his masterpiece, *Titan*, followed by two German novels, *Siebenkäs* and *Walt and Vult; or The Twins;* we shall also consider his last comic novel, *The Comet*. We will conclude with the treatment of one of his theoretical works, *Levana; or The Doctrine of Education*.

I am indebted to Professor Dr. Eduard Berend for permission to use the Jean-Paul-Archiv in Marbach/Neckar and for his patience in answering my questions. I am grateful to Mrs. Nancy Johnsrud and Dr. Elisabeth Boise for their suggestions and criticisms, and to Dr. Ilse Reis for helping me with the bibliography. Finally I should like to thank the Atlantis-Verlag for giving permission to quote from Emil Staiger, *Meisterwerke deutscher Sprache aus dem neunzehnten Jahrhundert*.

D.B.

Contents

Preface

Chronology

1. Biography   17
2. Idyllic and Humorous Stories   28
3. The Early Novels   38
4. *Titan*   55
5. *Siebenkäs*   83
6. *Walt and Vult;* or *The Twins*   96
7. *The Comet*   126
8. *Levana;* or *The Doctrine of Education*   131

Epilogue   150

Notes and References   151

Selected Bibliography   160

Index   173

Chronology

The length of the chronology is due to the great number of Jean Paul's works. Since only a fraction of the total work can be discussed in the text, it seems advisable at least to list most of the titles so that the reader will understand the wide range of Jean Paul's interests and be duly impressed by his indefatigable capacity for work. The witty formulation of the titles—contrast, paradox, metaphor—is significant for this author's style. His essays on literary criticism, a collection of which was published in 1825, are omitted. Long titles are abbreviated. Works that were not published in Jean Paul's lifetime show the date of composition in brackets.

1763   March 21: Birth of Johann Paul Friedrich (Fritz) Richter, the first son of Johann Christian Richter, deputy clergyman and organist, and of his wife, Sophie Rosine, née Kuhn, in Wunsiedel (Fichtelgebirge).

1765   Jean Paul's father is promoted to a ministry in Joditz, Saale.

1767   His father becomes a minister in Schwarzenbach, Saale. Jean Paul's mentors are the headmaster Werner and the chaplain Völkel, both in Schwarzenbach; and the minister Vogel from Rehau.

1778   Jean Paul begins to copy excerpts from his reading into notebooks.

1779   February: He enters the *Gymnasium* in Hof.
        April 25: Death of his father; beginning of his friendship with Johann Bernhard Hermann, Lorenz Adam von Oerthel, and Christian Otto.

[1780]   "Everybody Sets His Own Standards." He studies at home.

[1780–   "Exercises in Thinking."
1781]

[1781]   *Abelard and Heloïse*, a novel in letters. "A Word on Human Beings."

1781   May: He studies theology at Leipzig University, and is impressed by Ernst Platner, professor of philosophy.

[1781–   "The Praise of Folly."
1782]

1783   *Greenland Lawsuits* (two parts), published anonymously by Christian Friedrich Voss in Berlin.—Temporary engagement to Sophie Ellrodt in Hof.

[1783]   "Petition of German Satirists."

1784.   "Scattered Remarks on the Decline of Poetry."

[1784]   "Book of Prayers." "Answer on Contest on Theology and Poetry." "Meditations on the Apparition of the White Woman." "Discussion of the Objections Against the Existence of the Devil." "On the Godliness of Princes." Return to his mother in Hof.

[1785]   "Jokes in Quarto."

1786   Death of his friend Lorenz Adam von Oerthel.—"On World Religions." "On the Wigs and Black Gowns of Clergymen." *Mixtures for Men of All Ranks* (Essays written by Jean Paul and his friends, published anonymously.)

[1786]   "Praise of a Lady Who Swooned." "Stupidity Is Becoming to Simple People." "A Non-Christian Wise Man." "Some Well-Meant Admonitions Against the Stupidity of Going to Bed Only at Night." "The Year 1886."

1787   Jean Paul lives in the house of his late friend, Lorenz Adam von Oerthel, as tutor of the latter's younger brother.

1788   "What Death Is." "Murderous Philanthropy."

[1788]   "Description of My Epitaph."

[1788–   "Argument that Chastity Is the Lutheran Celibacy."
1789]

1789   *Selection from the Devil's Papers*, signed with the penname of J.P.F. Hasus.

[1789]   "Harlequin's Intermezzo." "The Bavarian Farthing-Comedy."

1790   Death of his friend Johann Bernhard Hermann. Jean Paul teaches in Schwarzenbach and founds the so-called "Erotic Academy" in Hof.—November 15: Vision of his own death.

Chronology

[1790] "Apology for Adultery." "Description of the Rooms in Which I Lived." "Concert in Saturnopolis." "Life After Death." "The Brewery of My Gastric Juice." "New Hypothesis on the Hypothesis of the Harmonia Praestabilata." "My Funeral Sermon at the Grave of a Beggar."

[1791] "Anthology of Wit." "New Year's Wishing-Hat."

1793 Jean Paul makes a trip to Bayreuth, Neustadt/Aisch, Erlangen.—*The Invisible Lodge*, signed with the penname Jean Paul. *Life of the Cheerful Schoolmaster Maria Wutz*. "Ringing out or The Seven Last Words." —Beginning of his fame as an author.

1794 Return from Schwarzenbach to his mother in Hof; he teaches and writes in Hof; second trip to Bayreuth, beginning of his friendship with Emanuel (Osmund); temporary engagement to Karoline Herold.

1795 "Victor's Essay on the Relation between the 'I' and the Organs." "On the Desert and the Praised Land of Mankind." *Hesperus*.

1796 Charlotte von Kalb invites him to Weimar. There he becomes a close friend of Herder and is introduced to Goethe, to the Duchess Amalia, to Knebel, and to Einsiedel. He meets Schiller in Jena and stops teaching.—"Speech of the Dead Christ." *The Trip of Rector Florian Fälbel. Life of Quintus Fixlein*. "Death of an Angel." "The Moon." "There Is No Selfish Love." "The New Year's Night of a Miserable Man." *The Pocket-Library*, published by his friend Th. Ellrodt, with the subtitle suggested by Jean Paul: "Flowers- and Fruit-Collection for Boys and Girls." *The Written Complaint of Bailiff Josuah Freudel*. "The Double Sacred Oath of Reformation." *Biographical Recreations Under the Skull of a Giantess*.

1796– *Flower, Fruit, and Thorn Pieces* (*Siebenkäs*).
1797

1797 Death of his mother. He accompanies his brother to Leipzig and acquires the new friends Friedrich Benedikt von Oertel and Paul Emil Thieriot. Emilie von Berlepsch plays a crucial role in his life.—*The Valley of Campan. Explanation of the Woodcuts Under the Ten Commandments in the Catechism*. "The Beggars

Are the True Bards." "History of My Preface to the Second Edition of Fixlein." "Gravamen of German Companies of Actors." *The Parson in Jubilee.* "Eclipse of the Moon."

1798 May: Accompanied by Emilie von Berlepsch, he visits Dresden, where for the first time he is confronted with classical art. He meets Karoline Schlegel.—July: Trip to Halberstadt, where he visits Gleim.—August: Second trip to Weimar.—October: He moves to Weimar; trips to Erfurt, Eisenach, Hildburghausen, Rudolstadt.—*Palin-Genesis.* "Privileged Last Will for My Daughters."

1799 He receives the title of Privy Councillor; engagement to Karoline von Feuchtersleben.—*Letters and Imminent Curriculum Vitae (Conjectural Biography).*

1800 May–June: Trip to Berlin; friendly relations with Josephine von Sydow, Henriette von Schlabrendorf, Rahel Levin. Queen Louise of Prussia invites him to the court in Potsdam.—October: He moves to Berlin. In the house of Henriette Herz he associates with Fichte, Schleiermacher, Tieck, Friedrich Schlegel, Bernhardi.—Engagement to Karoline Mayer.

1800 "Description of the Libraries of the Village Hukelum." "Sermon in Homage of the Sun Before and During His Accession to the Throne." *Clavis Fichtiana.*

1800– *Titan.*
1803

1800– *Comic Appendix to Titan.*
[1800 *Vita-Book.*
ff.]

1801 May 27: Marriage to Karoline Mayer.—June: Honeymoon in Weimar; the young couple settle down in Meiningen; friendly relations with the Duke Georg von Meiningen; visits by their friends Christian Otto, Emanuel, Thieriot, Charlotte von Kalb.—"Secret Lamentations of Modern Men."—*The Logbook of the Balloonist Giannozzo.* "D. Fenk's Funeral Sermon on the Stomach of the Prince of Scherau"; a satire to be published in the *Appendix to Titan.* This publication was forbidden by the Berlin censorship.—"July 17, or Charlotte Corday." "The Marvelous Company During New Year's Night."

1802	September 20: Birth of Emma, his first child.—"On Death."
1803	June: The family moves to Coburg, where they spend their happiest year.—November 9: Their second child, Max, is born.—December 18: Herder's death.—"Reasons Why the Author Does Not Deliver His Contribution to the Pocketbook."
1804	August: They move to Bayreuth, where Jean Paul stays for the last twenty-one years of his life. November 9: A third child, Odilie, is born.—"Request for Unhappy People." *Introduction to Esthetics.*
1804– 1805	*Walt and Vult; or The Twins.*
1805	*Booklet of Freedom.* "Habitual Cheerfulness." "Antiphony of Oreads and Naiads"; performed in honor of the king of Prussia and the queen, at the Luxburg in Wunsiedel, on June 14, 1805.—"Wishes for Luther's Monument."
1806	Fichte and Prince Paul von Württemberg come to Bayreuth to pay Jean Paul a visit. "Sermon of Peace for Germany." "The Good Luck of Being Deaf in the Left Ear."
1806– 1813	Prince Dalberg guarantees Jean Paul a regular yearly income.
1807	*Levana; or The Theory of Education. Supplementary Pages to Levana.* "Valedictory Address of the Morning-Paper"; humorously written for the inauguration of the journal.—"A Reader's Torments Brought on by Literary Sayings." "Various Prophetic Ideas." "Cautions Against Accidents." "Eleven Polymeters on the Last Day of 1807"; eight of these were incorporated into *Walt and Vult; or The Twins.*
1808	Savigny, Varnhagen, and Bernhardi visit Bayreuth.—"Ideas on a June Night." "Pasquinade on the Most Beautiful Woman Living at the Present"; a satire that had been rejected by the *Journal des luxes et des modes* in 1790. Jean Paul revised it.—"On the Newly Invented Art of Flying of Jacob Degen."
1809	"The Dream of an Insane Woman." *Army Chaplain Schmelzle's Journey to Flätz. Dr. Katzenberger's Jour-*

ney to a Spa. "Written Petition to the Planet Mercury." "The Devil's Confession to a Politician."

1810   The brothers Wilhelm and Leopold von Gerlach visit Jean Paul in Bayreuth. He makes a trip to Bamberg, where he meets E.T.A. Hoffmann.—*After-Twilights for Germany.* "My Sojourn in St. Nepomuk's Church." "Globe Relations." "The Weekday's Club Made Witty and Angry." "Some Fragments of the Mirror of Married Life," maxims from the planned description of Siebenkäs's second marriage.

1810–   *Fall-Flora,* a collection of articles published previously
1820   in the *Morgenblatt* and the *Damenkalender.*—"Fifth Request to the Readers of My Fall Flora."

1811   E.T.A. Hoffmann pays him a visit. Jean Paul makes a trip to Erlangen.—"Request Not to Impoverish Me Through Gifts." "Parental Love for Children, a Simple Story."

1812   Trip to Nuremberg, where he meets Friedrich Heinrich Jacobi, with whom he had exchanged enthusiastic letters since 1798.—*Life of Fibel.* "Penitential Sermon on Prepayments of Wolke's Work." Christian Heinrich Wolke (1741–1825), a grammarian and reformer of the German language, published his fundamental work, *Introduction to the German Common Language,* in 1812.—"Sphinx Moths or Sphinxes." "On the Author's and the Priest's Ethics."

[1812] *Via Recti.*

1813   "Reminiscences of the Best Hours of Life for the Hour of Death." "Death Poems."

1814   No trip, no visitors, as a consequence of the war; but thirteen publications because of his financial difficulties after Prince Dalberg's abdication.—"Remarks on Men." "The Origin of Dreams." "Question on the Origin of the First Plants." "Night Thoughts of the Accoucheur Walter Viermeissel." "Mars and Phoebus Exchange Thrones." *Museum* (collection of essays). "Conjectures About Some Miracles of Animal Magnetism." "Dispassionate Presentation of the Reasons Why Young People Rightly Expect from Old People the Respect Which the Latter Formerly Required from Them." "The Beauty of

Dying in the Prime of Youth." "Why Are No Cheerful Memories as Beautiful as Those from Childhood?" "Seasonable Observations During Europe's Month of May."

1815   Ferdinand Grimm and Henrik Steffens, a natural philosopher from Norway, visit Bayreuth.—"A German Youth in the Night of October 18." "Seven Final Remarks Against Pirated Editions." "A Suggested New Word for Lie"; the publication of the article was forbidden in Württemberg, but Voss published it in Leipzig in the *Zeitung für die elegante Welt*. "The Little Considered Danger of Winning a Lottery."

1816   Princess Katharina Paulowna of Holstein-Oldenburg, Count Schaffgotsch, and President Heim from Meiningen come to see him. He makes a trip to Regensburg, where he pays his respects to the Princess of Taxis, sister of Queen Louise.—"The Always Correct Meteorologist." "Dialogue Between the Two Faces of Janus." "Indian Summer Birds." "Note of Rector Seemaus on the Probable Destruction of the Earth on July 18 of this Year (1816)."

1816–   *Selina*.
1825

1817   Jean Paul's "Indian summer": He receives his honorary Doctor's degree in Heidelberg; finds a new friend, Heinrich Voss, Jr., and a devoted lover, Sophie Paulus.— "Philanthropist's Woodland." "Political Lenten Sermons." "Preliminary Report on the Sick- and Section-Report."

1817 ff. "Against Super-Christianity."

1818   Second trip to Frankfurt/Main and Heidelberg. In Frankfurt he meets Karl August Baron von Wangenheim, a politician and friend of Thieriot and of Friedrich Schlegel.—*Autobiography*, three lectures.

1819   March: Death of his friend, Friedrich H. Jacobi. Trips to Stuttgart and Löbichau, at the invitation of the Duchess Dorothea of Kurland.—"Dream of a Bad Spirit." "On the Evergreen of Our Sentiments."

1820   He visits his son Max, who studies classics and theology in Munich. He is admitted to an audience with King

Max Joseph of Bavaria, and is elected honorary member of the Bavarian Academy. Meets an old friend from Gotha, the archeologist Schlichtegroll.—"Against Titular Councillors." "Dream upon the Universe." "On German Compounds."

1820–1822	*The Comet.*
[1820]	"Against Morning Visits to Scholars."
1821	April: Trip to Bamberg. September: Death of his son Max.—"Disconnected Thoughts Before Breakfast in Löbichau." "Visions of a Greek Mother."
1822	Trip to Dresden, where he visits Tieck, Böttiger, his brother-in-law, Mahlmann, Helmine von Chézy.—"The Worshipers of Lucifer and Hesperus." "Political and Poetical Medley."
1823	Trip to Erlangen and Nuremberg.—"Marriage of the Two Highest Powers on Earth."
1824	Trip to Nuremberg.
1825	Fourth trip to Nuremberg; Chapter 5 of *Selina* finished. —Three introductions to other author's works, among them E.T.A. Hoffmann's *Fancies in Callot's Manner.*— A Short Postscript to the *Introduction to Esthetics*, containing the important chapters on Greek and Romantic Poetry, on Humor, Wit, Characters, and the Novel.— November 14: Jean Paul dies.

CHAPTER 1

Biography

SEVENTEEN complete and fourteen partial Jean Paul biographies have been published since 1817. In this biographical chapter, I shall refrain from combining the different aspects of his life described by my predecessors but shall rather take the facts and dates from the best organied text, Eduard Berend's introduction to *Jean Pauls Werke*,[1] adding passages from *Wahrheit aus Jean Pauls Leben* (Breslau, 1826-1833), and some unpublished material, notes on his students and his own children, that show him as a teacher and as a father.

Johann Paul Friedrich Richter was born, a few days after the end of the Seven Years' War, on March 21, 1763, the oldest son of a Lutheran minister and a born musician, who had married the daughter of a well-to-do merchant in Hof. Sophie Rosine, Jean Paul's mother, was a delicate, fairly unintelligent, and completely uneducated person. His native town, Wunsiedel, belonged politically to Bayreuth, subsequently to Prussia, and finally to Bavaria. The atmosphere was far from being cosmopolitan; everything was narrow, patriarchal, and conventional.

In the unfinished autobiography, where Jean Paul assumes the role of a professor of history lecturing on Jean Paul's life, the birth of little Fritz is described in a different, Jean-Paulish way:

It was in the year 1763, about the same time with the Peace of Hubertusburg, that the present Professor of his own history came into the world; in the same month that the golden and gray wagtail, the robin-redbreast, the crane, the redhammer, appeared, and many snipes and woodcocks arrived also; and, indeed, on the same day of the month, in case anyone should wish to strew flowers upon the cradle of the newborn, the spoonwort and aspen hung out their tender blossoms—on the 21st of March; also at the earliest and freshest time of day, namely, at half past one in the morning. But what crowns all is, that his life and the life of the spring began at the same moment.[2]

One day, when the poet was still a very small child, he had a crucial experience. He stood in the door of the house, looking towards the woodpile on the left, when all of a sudden, like lightning, he saw himself for the first time as being different from the rest of the world: "I am I." Max Kommerell reminds us of Goethe's experience as a small child, when he wanted to adore the sun as his god. He built an altar and caught the first rays of the rising sun with a magnifying glass in order to kindle the incense, creating by this act a relationship between himself and the objects of the external world, but without his touching them, thus filling them with profound meaning. For Goethe the individual object had a value in itself; it was a symbol of the world as a whole. Jean Paul, on the other hand, in this decisive moment, when he found himself for the first time and forever after, saw himself as being apart from the world.[3] The humorist in the young Jean Paul destroys the object, so that it becomes a symbol of the disharmony of the world. For him, strange habits, odd people, and all curious phenomena were the customary and normal in this world.

Another important experience of Jean Paul's early childhood was the disillusionment at the transition from imagination to reality, the fact that dreams which come true lose part of their glamor and fascination:

When Paul on Xmas morning stood before the lighted tree and the lighted table, and saw this new world of gold and splendor and gifts lying around, and discovered and took possession of one rich gift after another, the first emotion that arose in him was not a tear, not even a tear of joy, but a deep sigh over life—in one word, the transition, the leap, or the flight (call it as you will) from the wild-swelling, sporting sea of Fancy, to the firm land, limited and limiting—this transition the boy expressed with a sigh for a greater and more beautiful land.[4]

For the same reason, he preferred autumn and winter to the other seasons, because they gave him "domestic joys" and "poetic prospect sketching. . . . The widely extended plans of summer journeys and summer harvests are anticipated and enjoyed, and when the spring itself arrives, the chief business is already over."[5]

Jean Paul liked to make fun of himself as "the good domestic fool" having a "corner-loving disposition," and also of his preference for "spiritual nest-making" and of his "foolish union of desires for near and distant objects: he became a domestic snail who withdraws contentedly and loves to live in the narrowest recesses of his house. Only he will sometimes open his snail shell sufficiently to thrust out his four feelers, not widely enough to spread them like butterflies' wings in the air, but to stretch them ten times higher towards heaven. . . ." [6]

Jean Paul was a typical self-taught man. A minister in a neighboring city allowed him to use his library, which consisted mainly of works of the Enlightenment. Thus he developed a heterodox and enlightened philosophy of life at an early age. He felt, however, that education should not be based on reading but rather on writing and speaking. Themes for papers should be taken from history or from the student's life: "Yet better than all subjects for themes are perhaps *none*. The youth will choose for himself, as he would a beloved mistress, the matter of which he is full, and with it alone he can create that which is vital. Leave the young mind in freedom with its time and its themes, as older writers require, and he will find, like the bell that rests upon the ground, his own reverberations undisturbed by your touch; it can emit no sound until it hangs untouched in the free air." [7]

In 1779 Jean Paul was sent to the *Gymnasium* in Hof, where he had difficulties adjusting himself to a large class, a large school, and a large city, after having led a more idyllic life in the country. To his classmates he seemed like a being who had dropped from the moon; that is how Schiller described him later when he made his first appearance in Weimar. But Jean Paul won the respect of his classmates when, during a class discussion of Christ's godlike character, he contradicted the teacher so convincingly that the latter had no other way of saving his dignity than by ordering Jean Paul to keep quiet.

The compositions the boy wrote in school show common sense, a simple style, and his own phonetic spelling, which he did not normalize until his forty-first birthday. In 1781, his best friend in school, Lorenz Adolf von Oerthel, inspired him to write his first love story, *Abelard and Heloïse*, a description of Lorenz's love for Beata von Spangenberg, a neighbor's daughter. Jean Paul never planned to publish this story, whose "godfathers" were Goethe's *Werther* and Johann Martin Miller's *Siegwart* (1776)—the latter describing a sentimental love affair, which is broken off by a tyrannic father who forces his daughter to marry another man. Oerthel's beloved Beata also married another man one year after the completion of the novel. Since Werther writes letters to a friend, Abelard does the same, and he also shoots himself to death.

Only half a year later, Jean Paul criticized himself severely for his first opus, finding very few good passages in it. His intelligence was far more developed at this time than was his ability for creative writing, and he decided to follow Georg Christoph Lichtenberg's advice not to write a novel before the completion of his thirtieth year.

Jean Paul's father died before the boy graduated from the *Gymnasium*. He continued his studies at Leipzig University where he was not impressed by his professors. He preferred to read, on his own, "witty" authors like Seneca, Horace, Cicero, Voltaire, Pope, Swift, and Young. Inspired by the British satirists, he wrote *Greenland Lawsuits or Satirical Sketches*, for which he found a publisher in 1783. Jean Paul's early works are interesting because they show nothing more than his great intellect, cynicism, and bitterness presented in a brilliant style replete with witty and learned comparisons, as will be typical of his subsequent works. The source of these comparisons were excerpts from his reading. For three years he had collected in his notebooks striking facts, metaphors, and comparisons, arranging them under headings like: rich–poor, strong–weak, big–small, birth–death, etc. He could be sure to find impressive metaphors for any time and any occasion by simply going through his notebooks, which were full of the most interesting material.

One chapter of the book, a satire on authors, is so striking that no Jean Paul reader, publishing a book of his own, will ever dare to use a motto, a dedication, a fancy title, or dashes within a text, after having experienced Jean Paul's savage scorn for such things. Dashes, he says, are "furrows without seeds, algebraic symbols of subtraction, the skeleton of dead thoughts . . . , bridges crossing abysses of contradictory statements." [8] The title page is more important than the whole book. As long as it is glamorous, the title does not have to fit the contents of the book because, later on, only the title will be quoted in learned journals. Nor does the motto have to relate to the book. On the contrary, the less fitting it is, the more admiration the author will deserve for his brilliant mind which does not overlook the slightest similarity. In short, "Books are often nothing else but symptoms of a sick mind. I call the writing of a sermon, having diarrhea; of poetry, having a temperature; of book reviews, suffering from jaundice." [9] Jean Paul signed the introduction to this book simply "R," his first book being thus published anonymously.

After the publication of his first book Jean Paul went through a series of disillusionments. A second volume of the *Greenland Lawsuits* was published but went unnoticed. Consequently, the publisher refused to accept the manuscript of a third volume. In various law suits Jean Paul's mother lost all the money she had inherited from her parents and could no longer support her son, who left Leipzig in a hurry to escape his creditors. Potatoes became the Sunday meal for him and his mother; for they could hardly pay for their daily bread. However, in spite of all this misery surrounding him, Jean Paul used every minute of the day to improve his style, because he was convinced that he was predestined to become an author. He went on writing satires until finally, in 1789, he found another publisher in Gera who suggested *Selections from the Devil's Papers* as the title for the new collection of satires. This time Jean Paul used a pen name, J.P.F. Hasus. This second opus was less intelligible than the first one and received—if that were possible—even less notice.

In order to make a living, Jean Paul in 1790 went to Schwarzenbach, where he taught privately seven children from six to fifteen years of age. They loved him because he did not force them to memorize dates and facts but encouraged them, instead, to be creative. Among his literary remains is the handwritten *Anthology of My Students, 1791-1792*,[10] in the introduction to which Jean Paul says that he neither added to nor took away anything from these "Bons Mots" of his students.

Apparently the students were so impressed by their teacher's style that they adopted it completely. E.g.: Georg, eleven years old, writes: "In Portugal the climate of the earth is good, but not that of the inhabitants.— Winter sheds its skin when it loses the snow in spring.— A person who speaks half French and half

German is a language Creole." Leo, fifteen years old, states: "The body is the coat of the soul.— The human face is sometimes a blue sky, sometimes a dim one." Fritz, seven years old, quips: "Man is stuck in death like the snail in the shell," and Samuel, ten and a half years old, remarks: "Man consists of feelers.— My exam is my parents' doomsday.— Men like to go after electricity, like metals." Here Jean Paul adds rightly: "Les beaux esprits se rencontrent, I have the same comparison in MY book on page 183."

Discipline was no problem for Jean Paul. He put down twenty-one school regulations, all of them simple and logical: e.g., "1) he who remains outside for too long may not leave the classroom next time at all; 2) he who misbehaves on the way home will have to go alone for a whole week; . . . . 8) he who does not listen when I tell a story is sent home; . . . . 17) every morning I make sure that they have their hankies; . . . and 20) he who hits somebody will be hit himself."

The Sundays Jean Paul spent in Hof as the guest of well-to-do bourgeois people, like the postmaster, the mayor, rich merchants, the fathers of charming, intelligent daughters. He was in love with all of them. For him there was no basic difference between friendship and love, love being just a deeper feeling than friendship. He called his feeling for all these lovely girls his Tutti Love and their meetings the Erotic Academy. All of them married respectable men who were able to support a family. For a short time Jean Paul was engaged to one of them, Karoline Herold. But since she felt that he did not love her as an individual, and that whatever he felt for her he felt not with his senses but only with the power of his imagination, she was wise enough to give him his freedom.

On November 15, 1790, Jean Paul had a vision which affected him profoundly. He saw himself as dead, saw his lifeless hand hanging down from the bed, and in that moment gained an insight into the transience of human life and values. He promised himself to love all his fellow creatures, who had only such a short time to enjoy their lives. He had already experienced a similar feeling on the day of his confirmation.

I left the altar with the purity and the infinity of heaven in my heart. But this heaven manifested itself in me through an unlimited, gentle love, which no fault could impair, which I felt for every human being. The recollection of the happiness I felt, as I looked upon all the churchgoers with love, and took them all into my heart, have I preserved till this hour, living and fresh in my memory. . . . Every festival is followed by a working day; but we go from the one fresh-clad to the other, and the past leads us again to new ones. These spring festivals of the heart became, later, in the years of youth, only calm cheerful Sabbaths, when for the first time the ancient great stoical spirits, from Plutarch and Epictetus and Antoninus, appeared before me and took from me all the pains of earth and purified my heart from all anger. From these Sabbaths I hoped perhaps to have brought together a whole Sabbath year, or to have borne on with me what belonged to them.[11]

After this conversion of November, 1790, Jean Paul changed the content of his writing: instead of satires he wrote idyllic stories, among them the famous *Life of the Cheerful Schoolmaster Maria Wutz* and his first novel, *The Invisible Lodge,* which was published shortly before his thirtieth birthday. The publisher advanced him one hundred ducats, which enabled him to make life easier for his hardworking mother, who earned some money by spinning. Jean Paul introduced his new pen-name, JEAN PAUL, to the public, honoring JEAN Jacques Rousseau with the French pronunciation of his own first two names. But since his German readers did not understand, and pronounced PAUL the German way, Jean Paul gave in: he even spelled PAUL with gothic letters until he finally combined pen-name and his real name and called himself JEAN PAUL FRIEDRICH RICHTER.

Twenty-one months later, in 1795, he published his second novel, *Hesperus,* which made him famous all over Germany. Lavater had his portrait painted, and Charlotte von Kalb, Schiller's friend, invited him to Weimar, where Wieland and Herder were enthusiastic about his anti-classical style, whereas Goethe and Schiller were reserved, although polite. From now on, Jean Paul could afford to devote all his time to writing. He stopped teaching entirely, and after the publication of his third novel, *Siebenkäs* (1796/1797), he seemed to be well prepared to begin his masterpiece, *Titan.*

In 1797, Jean Paul's mother died. He left Hof, where he had shared a single room with her. He felt strongly that he stood at the beginning of a new chapter of his life. He was no longer an apprentice but rather a journeyman traveling through Germany for seven years, acquiring maturity as a man and mastery as a writer.

It is no wonder that the famous young author, who was extremely handsome and easily overwhelmed by attractive women, experienced some interesting love affairs. There was Emilie von Berlepsch, forty-two years old and about to be divorced, and Charlotte von Kalb, forty years old and willing to get a divorce in order to marry him; and there was Karoline von Feuchtersleben, a young and charming maid of honor at the court of Hildburghausen, to whom he was engaged for a short time. He even asked the Duke of Hildburghausen for a beautiful title, "Legationsrat," in order to impress the noble family of his fiancée. However, this did not work, and his and her doubts about the stability of their feelings caused a break and, once more, gave him his freedom. His most dangerous adventure was that with the beautiful, divorced countess Schlabrendorf, at the end of which he confessed to his friend that, although legally he could still consider himself a bachelor, actually he could not. Finally, in November, 1800, he became engaged a fourth time, to Karoline Mayer, the daughter of a judge at the High Court of Justice in Berlin, Johann Siegfried Wilhelm Mayer.

When Karoline Mayer met Jean Paul for the first time at a party in Berlin, "the young girl's heart beat wildly as she saw the miraculous man approach her because, in her humble timidity, she was fearful of the great task of conversing with him." [12] Jean Paul's kindness changed her fear into confidence, which moved him so much that he presented her with the carnation he wore in his lapel. Two days later he paid a visit to Karoline's father. "The great man was now closer to her, but like a being that she considered with religious feelings. With this sentiment in her heart she kissed his hand." [13] There is no doubt that even for a romantic young lady around 1800 Karoline's behavior was somewhat high-strung. Although she lived in her father's house, she explained to him in writing what she felt for Jean Paul because "she had no strength left for speaking." [14] The father was happy to agree to Jean Paul's and his daughter's wishes and grew only a little nervous when Jean Paul kept postponing the wedding for half a year.

24

Finally, on Whitsunday, 1801, they were married, the way Jean Paul had described it in advance in his *Conjectural Biography* (1799). In spite of her sentimentality, Karoline was an excellent housewife and a highly educated young woman. The newlyweds spent two glorious weeks in Weimar and two happy years in Meiningen where, on September 20, 1802, their first daughter, Emma, was born. Little Emma and a Pomeranian dog made Jean Paul completely happy. The year 1803, in which his son Max was born, was one of the happiest of his life. His two most harmonious works were written during this time: the novel *The Twin Brothers* and the *Introduction to Esthetics*. In 1804, shortly before his third and last child, Odilie, was born, he moved to Bayreuth, to which he was attracted by his friends Emanuel Osmund and Christian Otto, as well as the local beer.

Jean Paul had changed during his married life. He was no longer the ethereal youth adored by young girls and romantic women; he was now rather fat. He lived like a bachelor, thus giving his wife considerable anxiety. She tormented him occasionally with her jealousy, her complete lack of humor, and her idea about the upbringing and education of their three children, which differed altogether from his own. Some of these experiences certainly helped to shape the character of Lenette in Jean Paul's novel *Siebenkäs*. Among the unpublished preliminary notes for his *Levana; or The Doctrine of Education* we find some ideas that were perhaps inspired by Jean Paul's disapproval of his wife's way of handling the children, e.g., "Rather ceaseless teaching of a child than ceaseless admonition and fault-finding." Or: "I have always noticed that girls educated by men turn out to be paragons. Men give them clarity and strength, which women are unable to do. Girls brought up by men do not lose their delicacy of feeling, because in ethical matters a male teacher is as delicate as ethics itself. Men, especially young men, have as much delicacy as women, although they may not have the same respect for it." And: "Children have to be taught early —or they have to get rid of—everything that grows with the years like order, disorder, in short: ethics. However, walking, reading, knitting come without effort, by themselves and, besides, do not grow" (Capsule 10).

Besides the upbringing of their children there was another reason for Karoline to be, at times, rather nervous. She liked to keep the apartment neat and clean. Jean Paul did not care too much about this, and his animals even less. Before he went on a trip, he wrote down "Ten Commandments for Odilie," which give us an idea of what was going on in his room. Here are the first three: "1) Every Sunday you give six flies and fresh water to the frog couple; 2) The spider gets four flies each time Amoene [the wife of his friend Christian Otto, a regular visitor of the Richters] is here; she will remind you of the feeding because of the spider at her window; 3) Every morning you let the birds out of their cage, give them water for bathing and food for the day, and after one hour you put them back into their cage" (Capsule 10). Karoline was no friend of dogs and, therefore, was glad when her husband's pet ran away. His friends sent him two canary birds to fill the gap, but he had already bought a new dog. When the old one returned in the evening and a squirrel appeared, Karoline had an even larger menagerie to contend with.

In the morning, Jean Paul usually walked with his Pomeranian dog and his manuscripts to a small inn outside of the city, whose owner, Mrs. Dorothea Rollwenzel, was proud to offer him wine and the privacy and peace he needed for his writing. In the afternoon, he liked to stay home, reading, seeing friends and famous guests, among them Fichte, Savigny, E.T.A. Hoffmann, and Schelling. During the summer months, he liked to travel by himself to Bamberg, Nuremberg, Regensburg, Frankfurt, Stuttgart, Munich, Dresden, and especially to Heidelberg, where he spent the summers of 1817 and 1818. Voss, Jr., the son of the famous translator of the *Iliad* and the *Odyssey*, who was then a young professor at Heidelberg University, was instrumental in obtaining an honorary doctor's degree for Jean Paul. Sophie Paulus, twenty-four years old and the daughter of Heinrich Paulus, a professor of theology, attracted him greatly, to such an extent that he fell in love with her. Her interest in him and the students' admiration—they honored him with a torchlight parade—filled him with joy. Naturally, his wife became jealous of Sophie Paulus, and there were dark days when Jean Paul vaguely thought of getting a divorce.

JEAN PAUL FRIEDRICH RICHTER

Jean Paul's political writings were the result of his strong democratic feelings. As a young man, he had been inspired by the French Revolution. In spite of his connections with the high nobility, he wrote his *Booklet of Freedom* in 1805, asking for freedom of the press. In his *Sermon on Peace* (1808) and *Twilights for Germany* (1809), he tried to give courage and self-respect to his compatriots during the Napoleonic wars. His religious writings were published mainly after his death. In *Against Super-Christianity*, he championed a cheerful Christianity, free of dogmas. During the last nine years of his life he worked on *Selina*, an expression of his belief in life after death—a subject which he had discussed more than twenty years before in *The Valley of Campan, or Discourses on the Immortality of the Soul* (1797).

The last four years of Jean Paul's life were overshadowed by his son's death in 1821 and by that of young Heinrich Voss in Heidelberg. Jean Paul's friendship with Emanuel and Christian Otto cooled off in the twenties. His blindness, brought on by cataracts, made him completely dependent on the help of others. He died on November 14, 1825, one day before the thirty-fifth anniversary of the night on which he had seen himself dead.

CHAPTER 2

Idyllic and Humorous Stories

I Life of the Cheerful Schoolmaster Maria Wutz

WHEN Jean Paul chose the genre of the idyll after having written his satires, he was certainly under the influence of Rousseau and Herder, who had glorified the state of nature and the "natural man" above the blandishments of civilization. Jean Paul imitated, not the bucolic form of the original idyll, but the spirit and the philosophy of the earlier period. He described lower middle-class persons as simple people without idealizing or endowing them with heroic passions and tragic conflicts. Certainly he was aware of the split between reality and the ideal, but he presented it with humor and left no question as to his fundamental attachment to reality.[1]

Jean Paul wrote his idylls several years before Schiller defined the genre and presented a theoretical framework for it in his essay *Naïve and Sentimental Poetry* (1795-96). Schiller's definition took the term in its broadest sense as a harmony between Nature and Art, or the Ideal and Reality, wherein Nature and the Ideal embody joy and happiness. The intent of the idyllic poet is to show human beings in a state of harmony and peace with themselves and the world around them. This was possible at the beginning of civilization when mankind was not aware of the chasm between the ideal and reality. Eventually, Schiller felt, man would return to this primitive harmony, but until then, idyllic writing was possible rather on a "sentimental" level, i.e., in the knowledge that this harmony does not exist.[2]

For Jean Paul the idyll was not a description of the lost Golden Age. According to his definition in the *Introduction to Esthetics*, men can attain complete happiness, a modern Golden Age, by some form of renunciation, of property, intellectual values, social rank, or all three of these. For instance, Robinson Crusoe on his island and Rousseau on Peter's Island represent perfect idylls. A coachman driving along a good road on a sunny day denotes an idyll; he need not even meet his betrothed at the inn where he will enjoy a hearty meal. The baptism of the first child typifies an idyll—a happiness which any average person can experience. The idyll does not present major events and emotions but only "light small rainclouds," so that the reader is rocked gently up and down, floating without fatigue like the well-balanced characters of Jean Paul's idylls who live in a fenced-in garden, among flowers that seem to them like tall trees, as they do to Swift's happy Lilliputians.[3]

Among his own works Jean Paul mentioned as examples of genuine idylls *Wutz, Fixlein,* and *Fibel.* He was right to a certain extent; however, he put too much of his own life into his idylls, changing the genre almost into satire. For instance, when Wutz writes his own books to go with the titles he knows from catalogues—like Kant's *Critique of Pure Reason* or *Werther's Joys* (avoiding all sorrows, Werther's as well as his own) or some geographical work, leaving himself hardly a minute to talk to his son—we can guess at Jean Paul's self-pity, for he had always worked hard, making excerpts of everything he read, preparing himself carefully for his writing, all labors which in the end might turn out to be useless.

Wutz writes Klopstock's *Messias,* a difficult work and hard to understand, with a pen that produces illegible signs, this being his only way of producing a text that cannot be understood. This is no longer queer but plainly crazy, and in this way Jean Paul hints at the possibility of the uselessness of his own work.[4] At the end of the story, Wutz dies. The realistic description of this death, which Jean Paul took from the vision he experienced in 1790, is much too moving and exciting for idyllic poetry. Max Kommerell feels that an author may show us a dying hero, or a martyr facing death with greatness, whereas it is embarrassing, even almost indecent, to watch a comic figure—especially a grotesque figure like Wutz—facing death because he is not death's equal and is ineffectual and helpless.[5] But for us *Wutz* acquires its value precisely from the fact that the idyll is counterbalanced by the reality of death.

Friedrich Hebbel showed an understanding of Jean Paul's idylls, which mirrored the idyllic life of the author himself; he called *Wutz* the quintessence, the "succus" of Jean Paul's work.[6] Written in 1791, it was published in 1793 as an appendix to *The Invisible Lodge,* which perhaps explains its obscurity during Jean Paul's lifetime. Very few people read this little masterpiece, which became a favorite with German readers of the late nineteenth and the twentieth centuries. The story has hardly any plot because there is no problem to be dealt with. Wutz is sent by his parents to a good school in the neighborhood of his native village. He falls in love with a girl at home. After his father's death he takes over the latter's position as schoolteacher, marries his sweetheart, and is happy—not forever after, but until his death. The structure of the story is loose. There is a description of Wutz's childhood in the form of reminiscences by the old Wutz. This technique has been used before, but here these memories are constantly interrupted by premonitions, e.g., the description of his subsequent recreation of the books he cannot buy and of which he knows nothing but the titles. Later on, these books are used as sources for the description of his life, e.g., "Werther's Joys" for the eight happy weeks before his wedding. The description of the wedding is immediately followed by that of Wutz's death. On his deathbed he conjures up his earliest childhood memories as he fingers a baby cap and a small ring, which have special value for him.

There is absolutely no continuity in the narration of the story. The reader must be ready to reread a sentence more than once; he must concentrate on each word, grapple with metaphors, comparisons, allegories, and allusions; he must be willing to acquaint himself with names and facts belonging to all fields of knowledge. He will need dictionaries and encyclopedias; he must study the footnotes provided by the author and by subsequent editors. It is useless to ask why Jean Paul did not write in a simpler way. Apparently he could not express in an "easy" manner what he had to say. Since *ignorantia juris* does not protect a criminal against punishment, why should the *jus ignorantiae* of the reader prevent Jean Paul from having a style of his own? [7] He plays with words and images, willfully interrupts the story, creates and then destroys an illusion, and plays with us and the world of necessity since what he needs, above all, is freedom.

* * * * *

Eduard Berend calls *Quintus Fixlein* another Wutz belonging
to a higher social class.[8] Here Jean Paul limited the action to a
span of three years. He described life in Hof, a small town in
Bavaria, so openly that members of the faculty of the *Gymnasium*
complained and wrote a pamphlet against him. The main character in *Freudel's Lamentations* is an "Anti-Wutz," who, like Friedrich Theodor Vischer's famous character in *Auch Einer (One
More)* is a victim of the spiteful pranks of objects.[9]

The most appealing of Jean Paul's comic characters is
Schmelzle in *Trip of the Military Chaplain Schmelzle to
Flätz*, written in 1807 and published two years later. By virtue
of his imagination and an acute awareness of danger, Schmelzle
is a coward. We smile because we recognize in him a part of
ourselves, because potentially we are his cousins in cowardice.
The plot is not well rounded; for all events are connected simply
by the fact that they occur during Schmelzle's trip to Flätz. A
special oddity of this work is the vast number of footnotes that
have no connection whatsoever with the text.[10]

Dr. Katzenberger's Trip to a Spa was also published in 1809.
It is one of Jean Paul's "easier" novels, almost a comedy, skillfully
centered around Amandus Katzenberger, the typical scientist
with no feeling at all for poetry, sentimentality, or love. He is
an arrogant, coldly analytical doctor, a collector of abnormalities,
who could not quite forgive his wife that their daughter was
born without the slightest abnormality. Could she not have at
least two heads? Jean Paul's friends in Jena, among them Tieck,
were disgusted by the novel.[11] But whereas they resented Dr.
Katzenberger's attitude, we are inclined to enjoy his absurdities
and find his extreme cynicism exhilarating.

II Life of Fibel

Wutz, Jean Paul's first idyll, was, in a sense, a forerunner of
Fibel, his last one, except that Fibel turned out to be a mystic,
"perhaps the only genuine mystic of our classical literature." [12]
After the completion of his theoretical works and a break of
three years in his fiction writing, Jean Paul was longing for wit
and humor, for satire and idyllic scenes. The hero of his new
tagonist of the *Flegeljahre*, and of "Ehrgeck," [13] an odd German

31

epithet for a person who is vain, naïve, and eager to gain recognition and fame by any means. Jean Paul was disgusted with the grossly exaggerated praise meted out to Schiller and Kant by their biographers. These really great men, he felt, did not need to be popularized by an exposure of their private lives. Borowski, Kant's biographer, was even prepared to publish his work before Kant's death. The philosopher prevented this publication, but he could not keep people in Leipzig from meeting regularly to collect and discuss details of his life.[14] It was these facts that inspired Jean Paul to write a parody on vainglorious authors, but most of the material came from his own life and experience. The joy of a book's conception, the agony and despair before the first page is written, the problem of coping with too much or too little material, the feelings of exaltation at the sight of the first printed page, the chagrin when a hostile critic tears the masterpiece to pieces—Jean Paul experienced all of these, as does every author, who will feel that he is looking into a mirror when he reads the central ten chapters (eighteen to twenty-eight) of *Fibel*.

The work is divided into three parts, the first and last being idylls (or: the two halves of an idyll), and the middle part a straight satire. The three parts are linked by the central figure, Fibel, whom Jean Paul makes the author of an anonymous primer used in German schools and from which Jean Paul himself learned to read and write. It presents the letters of the alphabet in script and in print and exemplified in couplets for mnemonic reasons. It was also illustrated. The couplets are naïve and sometimes downright stupid; even the spelling and the syntax are not faultless. But Jean Paul describes the creation of the couplets as if they were equal to Milton's *Paradise Lost* or Dante's *Divine Comedy*.

A dream inspires Fibel to undertake his immortal works; in it he is riding backwards on a rooster who crows like the cock who warned St. Peter. In biblical accents a voice from heaven orders Fibel to pick a quill from the rooster's tail and begin his work. This heavenly inspiration enables him to create, but only with great labor and after long deliberation. The first letter of the alphabet gives him much trouble. He would like to start with Adam eating the apple, but he cannot present him undressed, which, after all, he was before finishing his disastrous dessert. So he changes Adam into an ape or monkey: "Der Affe sehr possierlich ist/Zumal wenn er vom Apfel frisst," meaning: "The monkey is very funny/Especially when he eats an apple." [15] The last letters of the alphabet, X-Y-Z, cause the greatest difficulties because there are few words that start with them. But his genius helps him to find a solution: "Xantippe war 'ne arge Hur'/Die X mal X macht 100 nur," meaning: "Xantippe was a naughty whore/Ten times ten gives only 100." An imaginary critic in the idyll reproaches Fibel with having ruined Xantippe's honor. Fibel will never be able to meet and greet her in the other world after ruining her good name and giving children bad ideas about women.

The Z-couplet finally overwhelms one with its humorous idiocy: "Die Ziege Käse gibt drei Schock,/Das Zahlbrett hält der Ziegenbock," meaning: "The nanny goat gives three heaps of cheese/The billy goat holds the toteboard."

In the same work, Jean Paul presents a glorious parody of an "Academy," the president of which is Pelz, who is the editor and publisher of Fibel's immortal work. At a session of the Academy, Pelz and his colleagues, the bookbinder and the printer, praise the Apollonian clearness and brilliance of Fibel's couplets as if they were comparable to masterpieces like Goethe's *Iphigenie* or *Tasso*.

Besides the members of the so-called Academy we encounter Fibel's loving but somewhat hysterical mother, and Drotta, his sweetheart, who are both anxious to admire his work. Drotta relies on the reports of her future mother-in-law, because she is not allowed to see her fiancé for a whole year, since he is not quite fifteen years old and poor, while Drotta is only fourteen years of age. These two women do not criticize Fibel's work, although Drotta is bright and has sound judgment when people other than her father and Fibel or his mother are concerned.

The idyllic scenes of the first part are constructed around Drotta. She lives in the forest on a hill which Fibel patiently watches from another wooded hill when he is afraid to visit her. When they were children, Drotta liked to beat him. On his fifteenth birthday he pays her a visit, offering her as his gift some coffee and gooseberry ice in a medicine glass which he had bought the day before in the neighboring city. The ice, of course, melts before Drotta receives it, and she can either drink it or wait for the next winter when it might change back into sherbet. This birthday celebration is to be their last meeting before Fibel's sixteenth birthday. It is November, and he helps her to place berries in traps in order to catch the finches who are on their way to warmer countries.

Fibel and Drotta walk in opposite directions singing church hymns, each one a stanza, so that they will be able to find their way back to each other. The farther Drotta gets from Fibel, the more loudly she sings, so that he believes her to be near him. Something "sweet and heavy" fills his heart while he is listening to her song. Drotta, too, has tears in her eyes because his voice reminds her of that of her dead mother. In this extremely subtle and moving way, the two loving teenagers are united by nothing other than their voices. In spite of her longing love, the practical Drotta notices that Fibel has placed most of the berries outside the traps, a mistake which she immediately corrects. They sit down to a supper of coffee and bread, but Fibel cannot eat, as he is brooding over their uncertain future. Drotta caresses his arm gently from the shoulder down to the fingers. After supper she accompanies him on his way home, until they discern the lights of the village. In the moonlight, they can see the green winterseed and the glowing red of the foliage. Winter birds are arriving, summer birds leaving; they seem to rest on the silver mountains of clouds. All this fills their souls with longing and happiness; the moon shows a "glamor of love in her eyes, and all roses open on her face, and they sank into their first kiss without knowing how."

Although Drotta's father, a hunter, has forbidden them to meet for a year, even this year is filled with happiness. On Whitsunday Fibel watches Drotta in church "decorated like a goldfish." Even funerals mean happiness to them if he can admire her "in the beautiful night of her mourning clothes." When there is no opportunity to meet her, he uses his "optical rod," a telescope which carries the sun-red mountain, from which he had watched Drotta's home before, right into the middle of the village, giving his imagination the power to see everything in the hunter's house, to hear Drotta's voice and the birds in the woods. This idyllic existence—a happiness made perfect through resignation—is only disturbed by the hunter's objection to their marriage, even after the waiting period is over. Half a year later, however, he gives them his blessing.

So far, Jean Paul has consistently followed his definition of idyllic poetry in this first part of the story, which contains only one scene—the death of Fibel's father—described with a merciless realism sharpened by some humorous details. The old birdcatcher does not fit into his casket when he lies down in it before he dies. He realizes that the stingy carpenter has betrayed him. He pulls his cap over his face so that neither his wife nor his son should see him suffer. He curses terribly, which usually makes him feel better. In his agony, he squeezes his favorite bird, a canary, to death. Jean Paul's vision of his own death, experienced in 1790, is always present in his writings and gives his idylls like *Wutz* and *Fibel* a depth which is rather unusual for this genre.

The middle part of the story, the satire, offers scenes full of humor, even of burlesque, that remind the reader of the sixteenth century, when the digestive process was discussed with tireless amusement. Fibel delivers the first three copies of his freshly printed primer to the three little sons of the count, who invites him to a stag party where, for the first time in his life, he smokes a pipe. To the count's utter amusement, Fibel's facial contortions show all too clearly the effect of the tobacco. Finally, in order to prevent a catastrophe, the count orders a servant to accompany Fibel out of the room. The servant leads him to the library and to an old-fashioned big chair next to which a huge folio is placed. Fibel is ready to admire the book in spite of the internal turbulence when the servant opens the seat of the chair like a lid, and leaves him alone. Now Fibel understands the situation, and after a while he reappears at the party, pale but much relieved and able to finish his pipe. Jean Paul's nephew, Richard Otto Spazier, who spent some weeks as a guest in his uncle's house, tells a similar anecdote about the unusual use of books. In the secret and necessary room of the house, he found an interesting book with the first pages missing. He "used" it by tearing out pages at random, whereupon the book disappeared because Jean Paul wanted the pages to be used in proper sequence.[16]

The third part of the story, a pure idyll, shows Fibel as the oldest man on earth, the "millionaire of hours," [17] who has changed his name, so that curious visitors cannot find him. He has also changed his personality, because now he sees the short-comings of his book and understands how stupid he was to consider himself a learned man and a great author. He is now 125 years old; at the age of 100, he has experienced a rebirth, and has grown blond hair and strong white teeth again. He lives in the company of animals—a poodle, hares, birds, and bees—and plants fruit trees all around his house, because he cannot bring himself to throw away a pit. He decorates the trees with colorful glass bowls and enjoys the reflected world with its silver, gold, and jewel effects, which he calls his "color piano." [18] He also owns a hand organ, with which he accompanies himself as he sings simple hymns. He reads an illustrated Bible from cover to cover, not in order to forget the world, but in order to enjoy life, even more deeply, from the example of the Eternal God who is himself eternally born into this world. Nonsense, or profoundly meaningful? Jean Paul does not answer this question, but he shows us Fibel as if in an apotheosis: there is a rainbow in the Western sky, an aurora borealis in the East. Both meet at the zenith, and time and eternity are fused.

The style of *Fibel* is that of the "classical" Jean Paul. There are fewer footnotes; the digressions are logically motivated and comparisons less farfetched. The author even stops and wonders whether a certain metaphor is helpful for the understanding of the text or should rather be omitted. However, even in his mature age Jean Paul has not changed completely. He still plays with his reader, fools him occasionally, and enjoys his poetic license. During the sessions of the "Academy," for which the editor, the printer, and the bookbinder collect the minutiae of Fibel's life, he listens with his back turned to the speakers to save himself the embarrassment of the praise. All of a sudden, Jean Paul interrupts his narrative and tells his readers that he is now the biographer of the biographers, telling in reverse what he told us before in historic order, throwing himself "back into the finished chapters."

The material for Fibel's biography—told by Jean Paul who introduces himself as the narrator—is collected by children who purchase the pages for him in stores and households, where the precious story is used for wrapping up merchandise or by crafts-men for their work. The locales where the pages are found pro-vide Jean Paul with titles for the different chapters, e.g., Coffee Bag, Herring Paper, Cap—or Jacket—Model, Taylor's Paper Measurement, and Lantern Chapter. As in his other stories, the author is always present and frequently addresses his hero, Fibel, whom he desperately tries to find still alive, so that he may learn from him the end of the story and finish his book on him before the next book fair. Finally, he discovers Fibel and accepts a gift from him: Alert, a Pomeranian dog, "this superlative animal . . . a dog of honor—or a medallion—or his Evangelical Animal . . . his coat of arms . . . I still own the dog. . . . [Jean Paul adds:] He is scratching himself, all alive, on my sofa." [19] If the reader wants to find out more about him by paying Jean Paul a visit, Alert will probably bite him in the leg. Once more Jean Paul forces us to jump back and forth between the world of illusion and the real one, liberating us from gravity, transforming us into "Nachhopstänzer," dancers hopping along after him.

CHAPTER 3

The Early Novels

I The Invisible Lodge

AFTER finishing the idyll *Wutz*, Jean Paul immediately started to write his first novel, *The Invisible Lodge* (1791-1792, published in 1793), which is undeservedly neglected. In addition to having all the charm and freshness of a first work, it contains in a nutshell Jean Paul's more popular novels, *Hesperus* and *Titan*. When Jean Paul sent his manuscript to Karl Philipp Moritz, the author of *Anton Reiser*, he had the incredible experience of the young unknown author who, after having received twenty rejections from publishers, was now greeted enthusiastically by a famous writer as being "greater than Goethe." [1] The publisher Matzdorff sent him a contract and the sum of a hundred ducats, Jean Paul's first income from his writing. Contemporary critics praised the book for its wealth of imagination, feeling and wit, but were critical of its mannerism. [2] It was not a financial success; and the second edition was not published until 1821. Jean Paul's real fame did not come until the publication of his second novel, *Hesperus* (1795).

Jean Paul's first novel provokes various and complex reactions in modern readers. The protagonist, Gustav von Falkenberg, spends the first nine years of his life in a cave in the company of his teacher, a young Moravian brother, called Genius, and a young dog. This was the condition imposed by Gustav's grandmother before she would give her daughter the permission to marry. We are informed that Gustav spent the very first years of his life in superterrestrial rooms, and that Genius, changing day into night, carried his sleeping pupil into the sun, as the ant carries its eggs. However, the idea of a child growing up underground is so absurd and repugnant to the naïve reader that it does not help him to know that Gustav is happy because he

lives in complete peace, without desires, and surrounded by the
love of his teacher, who fills his young heart with admiration
for great men.

Günter Grass interprets this cave life positively; for him it is
allegory in a realistic setting. He was comforted by Jean Paul's
novel because he did something similar in *The Tin Drum*, placing the clearly allegorical central figure in an otherwise realistic
plot.[3] Bernard Boeschenstein points out the metaphorical sense
of this underground education, at the end of which a Second
Life begins, which remains, nevertheless, within the boundaries
of earthly life. Jean Paul tries to describe the dialectic between
the cave life, which must be cast off, and *real* life, which consists
of being in harmony with nature and all human beings.[4] For
Eduard Berend, the central motif of the cave was inspired by
Rousseau, who wanted to keep a child away from all the influ-
ences of its environment.[5]

When Gustav finally leaves the cave, he thinks that he is
dying. The earth appears to him as heaven, the rising sun as
God, and human beings as blessed spirits. Fritz Strich, referring
to the German Romanticists, on whom the *Lodge* made a lasting
impression, called this merging of two worlds "the Romanticist's
delight." [6] Originally, Jean Paul had planned to call his novel
A Romantic Biography, but his friend Christian Otto advised
him against it, since the German adjective "romantisch," derived
from "Roman," meaning novel, had been discredited in the
eighteenth century by the works of poor novelists. Five years
later, after the publication of the periodical *Athenaeum*, in which
the Schlegel brothers discussed their ideas on Romanticism, the
adjective "romantisch" was endowed with a new meaning, so
that the title *A Romantic Biography* would have had an immediate claim to be considered avant garde. Tieck, Novalis, E.T.A.
Hoffmann, and later on Brentano, were, in any case, deeply
impressed by this novel.[7]

The romantic transition from one world to the other is once
more experienced by Gustav in a dream about his first teacher,
Genius. He had missed him bitterly during the first night in his
parents' house when he was shaken by fever after the excitement
of the first day on earth. But the following morning, when he
was well again, he forgot his teacher like all children of his age

and his character. Only at night did he feel a longing for the friend of his early childhood. Some years later, before leaving home to enter a military school—where his father hopes he will become tough after the Moravian brother has made a "milksop" of him—he dreams that he has been changed into a dewdrop lying in a blue flower—the first Blue Flower of Romanticism—that grows and carries him into a high room where Genius stretches his arms towards him; but the arm drops off, the blue flower collapses, Genius is carried towards heaven, and Gustav wakes up standing at his open window. He calls to his friend asking him to return, to reveal himself, to let him die, at least to let him hear his voice. At this moment, he hears his name called close to the window, then repeated twice from a distance; and then reality and dream are fused.[8] Jean Paul subsequently mentions that most probably the talking starling, one of Gustav's former playmates, had called his name as he was flying around in the park. But it does not matter, the author says, whether states of high excitement are brought about by starlings or spirits.

In a special mission during his training as cadet, our hero enters the house of Mr. von Roeper, encounters the latter's angelic daughter Beata, and falls in love with her. His friend Amandus is very jealous, but on his deathbed he asks Gustav to love Beata more than him, and he joins Gustav's and Beata's hands. After his friend's death, Gustav mourns, standing next to the pyramid that adorns his grave. It is late at night. Half kneeling he falls asleep. Beata sees him, closely watches his happy face, carefully removes two pebbles that might hurt him in case he should fall in his sleep. She wonders whether the night air is good for him and decides to wake him from a distance, but as she is approaching him, a sudden loud organ note makes Gustav rise, grasp her hand and say, still half asleep: "Oh take me wholly, blessed soul! Now I have you, beloved Beata; I, too, am dead!"[9]

In his dream, Gustav had lain in the silver shadow of flowers which he could not leave; but he had seen "two bodies in the air dissolving into a thin evening cloud, and the falling cloud revealed two spirits, Beata and Amandus."[10] They could not touch him or enter the silver shadow, but the sound of the organ released him and he rose and grasped the real Beata's hand. Gustav thought that the dream had passed out of his sleep into reality and that he had not slept. . . . "Where are we," he said to Beata,[11] his dream still vivid to him. Beata trembled; she felt as if she were dying in his arms. Now his dream became reality, and he said: "Now we are dying." After this sublime moment "while he was the sole hearer of the organ, the only sound in the solitude, while he was the sole watcher in the circle of sleep," [12] Beata opened her eyes again, and the two lovers found themselves united in a new paradise. The line between dream and reality disappears, and the scene ends with a kind of *Liebestod,* one of the favorite motifs in German literature from Gottfried von Strassburg through Richard Wagner.

There are other romantic features in the *Lodge* besides the merging of dream and reality: the fondness for night scenes, dreams, mysticism, the stressing of the spiritual, the role of music, the subjectivity of the whole as compared to the objectivity of classical poetry.[13] The language is essentially romantic. The book also contains many sublime passages, poems in prose, like the dreams mentioned above. Jean Paul himself felt that he had been successful in describing Gustav's "Rising from the Death" (Fifth Sector), the love scene at the pyramid (Thirty-third Sector), and five "Sectors of Happiness," Beata's reconciliation with Gustav, towards the end of the unfinished novel.[14] Passages like these were selected and published by Stefan George, who discovered in Jean Paul the father of Impressionism.[15] It is interesting to note that some of these passages—descriptions of scenes and characters—were worked out in advance before Jean Paul decided about the plot, which was utterly irrelevant to him.[16] The plot is needed only to give the characters room for their development, because the novel is "a psychological history that grows, supported by the lacquered flower-stem of the exterior action."[17] In one of the introductions, "Introductory Speaker," Jean Paul ridicules the reader who demands a well-planned plot that is clearly recognizable already in the first volume. If the author tells the beginning in the middle of the story, returning from there to the "beginning beginning"[18] and presenting scenes and episodes as if they had been shaken up in a wild turmoil, he makes his reader angry.

Jean Paul wanted to provoke his readers further by calling the book *The Invisible Lodge or the Green Corpse Without the Ninth Nutcracker,* but his friend Christian Otto advised him against this.[19] Instead he shocked—or pleased—his reader by using certain features of second-rate literature, gruesome trivialities, cheap effects, and mysteries. Little Gustav, for instance, is kidnapped by a mysterious woman—perhaps his father's former mistress, since Gustav looks exactly like her own son Guido, who was also kidnapped years ago. Children are secretly exchanged; and we don't know whether Gustav is really Falkenberg's son, or whether he is the son of the prince, exchanged by Genius, and destined to inherit the throne. There are three portraits resembling Gustav; who are his doubles? When he was kidnapped, he was playing with his sister. Whose daughter was the little girl? The eyes of the little boy Amandus are gouged out by a wicked old woman who wants to use him to arouse pity while she is begging. Amandus is saved by Gustav's father and cured by Dr. Fenk, a physician who recognizes him as his illegitimate son, whose mother lives in Italy.

There are intrigues, jealousies, love stories, seductions: Gustav succumbs to the prince's elderly but experienced mistress; Beata resists the parallel attempts of the prince to seduce her. There is a political society, a group of conspirators meeting in a cave, to which Gustav apparently belongs and in which Ottomar, Gustav's counterpart and the prince's illegitimate son, plays a leading role. Ottomar has sworn never to reveal the secrets of the conspirators except in the last hour of his life. When the conspirators are discovered by accident and Gustav is imprisoned, Ottomar, before committing suicide, reveals everything to Dr. Fenk, in order to save Gustav. These exciting events fill three pages of the final chapter which ends, referring to Ottomar, "But he is still alive." [20] And this is the end of the novel, which was never finished.

There are some hints of further possibilities. Gustav is liberated because Genius, who looks exactly like his supposed half-brother, takes his place in prison.[21] Will the secret society educate Gustav, just as Wilhelm Meister was educated by the Society of the Tower, until he is ready to become the ideal political leader? Jean Paul does not enlighten the reader; most probably he had not yet decided how to develop the plot. Boeschenstein is right when he calls this plot an arbitrary dummy, a melodramatic thriller.[22] As if by contrast, the realistic plot seems to provide occasional glimpses of the mysterious fairy-tale characters who seem to come from nowhere.[23] They have no clear shapes. The same youthful heroes, noble women, aggressive or resigned humorists appear in all his novels with different names and slight variations. Baumann calls Jean Paul's work "poly-novel," or "Allbiographie,"[24] because Jean Paul represents himself in all his characters, splitting himself up in order to produce a multitude of characters who are all aspects of his own personality. In a similar way, Wutz produced all the masterpieces of great men by spinning them like a spider out of his own five spinning warts.[25]

In Gustav, Jean Paul presents his own youthful ideal. Other children call him stupid because he is not shrewd, or proud because he is not noisy.[26] He finds escape in his friendship with Amandus, who is as close to him as is humanly possible, a second ego living with the first ego "almost under the same roof." That is to say, he loves his friend more for his vision of him than for what he really is. Gustav's enthusiasm for nature is based, creatively, more on his vision of nature than on nature as a thing in itself. He is the moving representative of noble youth, "ein hoher Mensch," an ideal type Jean Paul discusses in a special chapter.[27] Such noble souls are capable of rising to transcendental worlds; they are willing to die for a great cause; they give love rather than take it; and they are always aware of the discrepancies between their ideal existence and earthly realities.

Beata is another noble soul leaning towards enthusiasm, sentimentality, and poetry. She is not like the average woman, whose best "medicine" is a new dress or who, deeply moved by Christ's preaching, would notice his vest and his socks. Her feeling of honor, an inborn self-esteem, gives full harmony to her character, her movements, and her speech. Gottfried von Strassburg describes the same ideal woman and praises the same concept of honor and self-esteem as proof of purity and essential nobility.[28]

Gustav's counterpart, as noble as himself, is Ottomar, a titanic character who wants to change the world, who would not mind being hanged if he had succeeded in overthrowing the despotic government. In his private life, he loves to be surrounded by youth, young animals, birds, and children as both companions and servants. This strange young man has filled his living room with life-size copies of his friends, which he decorates with black flowers when they have died, with fresh flowers while they are alive. He undergoes the experience, similar to Jean Paul's own dream, of appearing to be dead. When he comes back to life, he is sick of both life and death. He asks himself, "What are you? What is sitting here and remembers and suffers?" [29] He ceases to strive for the improvement of the world: "The two eternities tower up on both sides of our earth, and we creep and grub on in our deep narrow pass, stupid, blind, deaf, chewing, wriggling, without seeing any greater path than that which we plough with our chafer-heads into our own ball of dirt." [30]

The same strangeness, bitterness and nobility characterize Fenk, Jean Paul's first "humorist," who reappears as Schoppe in *Titan*, as Leibgeber in *Siebenkäs*, as Vult in *The Twins*, and as Giannozzo in the *Comic Appendix to Titan*. In outward appearance he is repulsive, with a birthmark on his temple shaped like the tails of two polecats. Although he criticizes mankind sharply, he is resigned to reality and can put up with individuals and even love them. He loses his patience only when he sees an evil deed; and then he despises the deed, but never the individual.

A discussion of Jean Paul's style offers the richest opportunity to know the author. Jean Paul destroyed the traditional shape of the novel, not only by doing away with formal plot and characters, but also by asserting his constant presence, by interruptions and digressions, by encyclopedic servings of information in announced and unannounced "Special Pages." It is well known that Laurence Sterne's *Tristram Shandy* was his model, that the plot, the characters, and the other traditional aspects of the novel provided him merely with a framework for his continuous conversation with the reader. A new era in Jean Paul scholarship began when critics began to interpret these digressions as structurally necessary, to understand the apparent diffraction as creative construction, and to call Jean Paul's unrestrained imaginative power carefully planned caprice.[31] Norbert Miller places Jean Paul solidly within the literary tradition of his time, when

the novelist had two techniques at his disposal: the strictly auctorial form in which the author is invisible and/or identical with
the protagonist, or Sterne's form of the anti-novel, in which the
storyteller is at the center of his creation, so that the motions of
his own intellect form the basic structure of the novel.[32] Jean
Paul does not slavishly imitate Sterne's technique; he creates a
form of his own and actually borrows from the traditional style.[33]
Even *The Lodge*, in spite of all the digressions, still has a kind
of plot, and the author and protagonist do not fully coincide.

The Lodge is the most extreme example of this new type of
anti-novel, and it is not surprising that the classicist Goethe did
not respond at all when Jean Paul sent him a copy of his work.[34]
Long discussions on education, on female popes, on adultery
and divorce, on the thumbs of reigning monarchs, etc., interrupt
the action, but not before the reader is so completely wound up
in the spider's thread that he can be dragged or thrown wherever
the author pleases. He warns the reader that not only a liar but
also a reader must have a good memory, because he must be
able to memorize the first ten or twelve chapters of a novel and
use them as a basic grammar and vocabulary; otherwise he will
never grasp the more advanced chapters without remedial lessons
from the author. But the average reader forgets and misunder-
stands everything and must be assisted by short summaries of
past chapters or by helpful hints such as: "Now the real story
begins," or "Attention please, there will be consequences for the
reader when I say . . ."[35]

Another confusion is created when the storyteller becomes an
actor in the story by changing "from the first to the third person."[36] Jean Paul is Beata's music teacher and falls in love with
her. But when he becomes Gustav's tutor he renounces Beata
because he will not compete with this handsome and deserving
rival. Jokingly he points out that he did not choose the role of
a tutor in order to "put into" Gustav what he plans "to get out
of him" for the sake of his book, because he could have chosen
the easier way of the average novel writer who uses his imagination and simply tells lies. But he claims to be writing a biography, not a novel.[37] Here he ridicules authors of his time who
refuse to call their works novels, but rather call it history, biography, or appendix, in contrast to baroque novels such as *The*

Grand Cyrus, Astrée, or *Cléli,* which were disliked for their
fantasy. The eighteenth century preferred realism and judged
fiction on the basis of how well it accorded with fact.[38] To com-
plicate matters even further, another character of *The Lodge*
also writes a novel with Gustav as protagonist. Jean Paul hopes
that this novel will be published before he finishes his book, so
that he can refer to it! [39]

We find direct imitation of Sterne's style in Jean Paul's report
of his illness, which takes nine chapters that grow shorter and
shorter, down to four and a half lines. Finally, his sister Philip-
pine takes over because Jean Paul is too weak to continue. He
suffers from strokes, phthisis, a lizard in his stomach and, most
seriously, from a growing gooseberry bush in his intestines.
Dr. Fenk diagnoses these symptoms as hypochondria and pre-
scribes motion for the body and rest for the soul, because the
emotions caused by creative writing are as harmful as thinking.
Boeschenstein calls this "biographical ego . . . hidden in different
costumes" superfluous because Jean Paul is omnipresent in his
novel; it is a technique by which he leads the "Polyhistor" *ad
absurdum.*[40] Brewer sees in Jean Paul's "toying with the subject"
an excellent example of romantic irony,[41] whereas Hugo von
Hofmannsthal finds in it a "saturnalia of the mind," a total confusion that can be disentangled only by the most patient of
readers. Our era, brought up on Valéry, Musil, and Benn, recognizes "Denkerschuetterungen" as the origin of Jean Paul's writing and places him far above Expressionism and Surrealism.[42]
From the Baroque aspects[43] through the Enlightenment[44] and
Romanticism[45] to modern trends in fiction writing, the reader
can find a wealth of opposing traditions in Jean Paul's work and
choose the line he likes best. Perhaps this is one of the reasons
why Jean Paul's literary image has changed so constantly.

All these profound esthetic interpretations do not mention the
unbearable sentimental scenes which build a barrier for today's
young readers, who cannot remain serious when Gustav is described as having a doll's face with pale pink cheeks, a deep
red upper lip, eyes blue like the open sky, under long eyelashes.
Beata's soul is the note of a nightingale hidden under blossoms,
her body a snowflake that lasts only in the air and dissolves
when it touches the earth. When Gustav is nine years old, his

favorite playmate is a black lamb which he leads by a red ribbon. Years later, when he is in love with Beata, he tells her in great detail about the black lamb with such fervor that she is deeply moved and cannot speak. During this conversation, they stand in an arched window of the castle under which the gardener's children, their little friends, play at making love to each other and pretend to be Gustav and Beata. The little girl gently caresses the boy's cheeks and arms. The boy, in turn, throws his arms around her neck so abruptly and awkwardly that his elbows stick out to the left and right of her head. This is too moving for Beata; she drops a rose intentionally or by accident. Gustav picks it up and returns it; and their eyes meet in a gaze that touches the soul.

Gustav's despair after losing his virtue in the arms of the prince's mistress seems almost ridiculous today. In a last letter to Beata he confesses everything. He knows that there is no atonement for him. He leaves her, his work and the city, and goes to live with his parents, having turned pale and silent. The following spring, Beata undergoes medical treatment in a small spa, Lilienbad, where her window is decorated with a single forget-me-not over which she "breathes a long evening-song into her chorded echo."[46] On her "tugendhaften Tag"[47] a tear tells Gustav that she still loves him. In her eyes he reads that her soul loves nothing but God and Virtue. The following example shows that Jean Paul is not ridiculing sentimentality but is perfectly serious; it is our attitude toward the expression of sentiment that is entirely different. Beata and Gustav weep with happiness at their reconciliation after Gustav's seduction:

Beata looked into his overflowing heart, and hers ran over into a tear and yet she knew it not; but when the tear of the holiest eye trickled down the rosy cheek and hung on that rose-leaf with trembling glimmer —when his locking and her locked hands could not wipe it away— when with his flaming face, with his too blissful, bursting heart, he was about to wipe the tear, and bent toward the fairest object on earth like a rapture bending toward virtue, and touched her face with his—then did the angel who loves the earth draw the two purest lips together into an inextinguishable kiss—then did all the trees sink out of sight, all suns passed away, all heavens fled, and Gustav held heaven and earth in a single heart clasped to his breast. . . .[48]

The tearfully sentimental image of Jean Paul appealed especially to the Biedermeier and Victorian periods of the nineteenth century, when he was interpreted as the idyllic poet living in a small, peaceful world of his own.[49] Jean Paul preaches virtue as freely as he expresses his emotions. To see our main aim in life as being good and noble, to change and renew mankind by cleansing oneself of any immorality—because all the evil in this world is caused by the immorality of a few—to feel responsibility and guilt for all the misery in this world: this side of Jean Paul was discussed in the twenties,[50] whereas our era is embarrassed even when a clergyman uses words like good and evil or virtue and guilt.

While Gustav represents Jean Paul's ethical ideal, Ottomar is the mouthpiece of his political ideas. The best way to help people, or to be their tribune, is by being an advocate who can take up the people's case against the prince. To live under a despotic monarchy means for his subjects "to cry, cough, pray, take laxatives, hate, urinate, everywhere at the same minute."[51] The prince who supports his shaky throne by additional taxes is cursed by Jean Paul because he is undisturbed by the complaints of the people, whereas he is greatly moved by the sigh of a beautiful lady. He hates his brother when the latter recovers after an illness, because now he will have to continue paying his appanage. He is unmoved by his son Ottomar's death; and his callousness proves that he has a prince's heart a petrifact.

Jean Paul dwells as freely and as extensively on his religious ideas as on his ethical and political attitudes.[52] Gustav feels one with the universe where the "lightning of love" creates all beings. "Das *Bild* des Urgenius"[53] is seen by him in all created things, but only man represents not the image but the genius himself. Gustav's "Traum vom Himmel" reflects Jean Paul's belief better than any theoretical discussion because the magic of his language is more convincing than the content. What a poet has to say can never be rendered by any words but his own.

He died, it seemed to him, . . . he sank into a tossing sea of blossoms . . . ; on the ground of immensity all stars bloomed white and neighborly blossom leaves tossed against each other. Why did this flower field growing from the earth up even to heaven intoxicate all souls . . . sunk down in bewildering ecstasy? Why did a juggling wind mingle souls together with souls and flowers amidst a snowflurry of sparks and many-colored flakes of fire? Why did so sweet a dream envelop deceased men?—O, for this reason . . . ; man, still bleeding from the blows of the former earth, was to be healed under the flowers for the future heaven where the greater virtue and knowledge demand a healthy soul. . . . When on every snow-field one soul embraced another, then out of love they walked into *one* glowing dew-drop; then it trembled downward and alighted on a flower, which breathed it up again, rent asunder, as holy incense. High over the blooming field stood God's paradise, out of which the echo of its heavenly tones, in the form of a brook, flowed down to the plain; its melody wandered through all the windings of the lower paradise and the intoxicated souls plunged in their ecstasy from the flowery shore into the streams of flute-music; and the resonance of paradise all their senses expired, and the two finite souls, dissolved into a bright tear of joy, floated on upon the running waves. . . . Then God gave the signal that he was passing by, and an immeasurable love constrained all souls in this lofty stillness to embrace each other, and none sank upon one, but all on all—a blissful slumber fell like dew on the embrace. . . .[54]

In "The Narrow Bridge of Art," Virginia Woolf describes the essence of the novel of the future as follows: "We have come to forget that a large and important part of life consists in our emotions towards such things as roses and nightingales, the dawn, the sunset, life, death and fate. . . . We long for ideas, for dreams, for imaginations, for poetry. . . . [The novel of the future] will give the relations of man to nature, to fate; his imagination; his dreams. But it will also give the sneer, the contrast, the question, the closeness and complexities of life."[55] She might as well have been describing Jean Paul's novels and his general views of man and metaphysics.

II Hesperus

In a way, *Hesperus* is a second, revised edition of *The Invisible Lodge*. This time we have the four illegitimate sons of a prince, all of them kidnapped, and three of them educated in England, famous for her liberalism. The brothers are brought up in Eton and London with the ambition to replace their father's evil advisers and to give the people justice and dignity. After their return from England, they blow up a powder magazine as a sign of the revolution. We also encounter legitimate sons; one fathered by the clergyman Eymann, another by Lord Horion, and even one sired by the prince; but none of them lives with his parents, and they are all mistaken about their origin. Shortly before his death, Jean Paul admitted that this exchange of sons must be frustrating for the reader.[56]

Hesperus also makes use of a secret political club, a saintly teacher, a pure and noble young girl, and two friends who are in love with her. But this time the story, which is a parody of an ordinary novel, comes to an end. The true lovers are united, the jealous friend turns out to be the brother of the girl, and he is released—he is believed to have killed the girl's father in a duel—because a mysterious lady, called from England, declares him to be her son by the prince, born in wedlock.

In the case of *Hesperus,* Jean Paul experienced the excitement of being the author of a best seller. The first edition appeared in 1795, the second in 1798, and a third in 1820. But this last edition sold slowly because Jean Paul's audience had changed after the Napoleonic wars and the Restoration. But by 1795 it had achieved a popularity which can only be compared with the enthusiasm generated by Goethe's *Werther.*[57] In the *Neue allgemeine Biblographie, Hesperus* was praised as the favorite book of all people with "pure hearts and deep feeling."[58] Jean Paul was blamed only for his "abundant excesses" and for his overly pretentious style.[59] Jean Paul's contemporaries enjoyed what he called his "revelry,"[60] his flights of sentiment, the highly dramatic moments, such as the saintly Emanuel's death, Victor's burial sermon on himself, Victor and Klotilde's love scene in an arbor during a rainstorm.

Here, even the modern reader who experiences no difficulties in enjoying Jean Paul's stylistic excesses, is willing to accept Jean Paul's "Schwelgereien": his concept of death, for instance, as extermination softened by his belief in God, the non-death. In *Hesperus,* this concept of death takes concrete shape in scenes and persons.[61] We also understand what Musil meant when he called reserves of thoughts the basis of treasures of feeling.[62]

The most striking figure in *Hesperus* is Emanuel, an Oriental reincarnation of the Genius and a portrait not of Jean Paul's later friend, but rather of K. Ph. Moritz, who died while Jean Paul was writing the chapter on Emanuel's death, without knowing about his patron's ill fate. One source of the Oriental theme he used here is a novel—*Dya-Na-Sore* by Meyern—based on fairy tales, which tells of four brothers who liberate their country and establish a republic. The other source, Forster's translation of Kalidasa's *Sakontala*, provided him with a model for Emanuel in the priest Kanna.[63] Pietism, eighteenth-century Germany's mystical form of Lutheranism, prepared the way to Indian philosophy, which was introduced by Herder and systematically discussed by Friedrich Schlegel in *On the Language and Wisdom of the Indians* (1808).[64]

One of Jean Paul's constant preoccupations was how to face death. Emanuel offers one solution, for he determines the day of his own death, lives knowingly and willingly towards it, and invites his former student, the young physician, Victor, to be present at it. He even asks him to accompany him to his open grave, into which he has sown flowers four weeks earlier, so that they should bloom on the last day of his life. The "great wisdom" he teaches his young friends is "I and you, all human beings, all angels and all little worms rest at the heart of the infinite Spirit, and the ocean of suns and worlds is like a child in his arm."[65] The light, color, men, and ideas, are all mirrors of God's love; he conceives us when we think of him. But even Emanuel, the prophet of mystical pantheism, experiences fear when the moment of his death, predicted for midnight, approaches, and eternity appears to him like an endless night in which nothing consoles him and nobody answers. When midnight passes, he grows impatient. At this moment the powder magazine explodes, and he is thrown unconscious into his open grave. Gustav and Julius (a blind boy who loves him like a father) believe him to be dead.

But this is not the end of Emanuel's suffering. After a thunderstorm, he recovers; the earth appears to him as Eden, and the moon as the distant earth. He dreams that God steps from His throne as a gentle breeze of zephyr. In an ecstasy of happiness, he greets Him: "This is you, All-Loving-One." At this seraphic moment, a maniac, who has cut off his left hand because he believed that death held him by it, passes by, bleeding, waving his hand, shaking his head at Emanuel and screaming: "Brrr! he has you, but not me! Nothing but mould is hanging on you! The eyes are gone! Brrr!"[66] Emanuel feels condemned. The next day, he blames himself for having made too much fuss about his death, and for having neglected life by putting too much emphasis on a future life, without gaining it. Towards evening, he once more

51

loses consciousness, and in the middle of a vision which shows him that all souls are destroyed by one great ecstasy—as was Jean Paul's personal conviction—he dies. His death is not caused by a philosophical decision but by pneumonia. It is this mixture of realism and mysticism which makes the ecstasy bearable.

A similar mixture of reason and passion, humor and sentimentality, realism and idealism characterizes Victor, who is a true image of Jean Paul himself, full of inner tensions, but laughing philosophically at death. He is not the pure humorist like Schoppe in *Titan* or Giannozzo in the *Comic Appendix to Titan*, because he loves the world, music, his work, and all beautiful girls. He is a court surgeon but hates all courtiers and career hunters. He is deeply in love with Klotilde who, at first, is shocked by his satirical remarks. But when she finds out that her adored teacher Emanuel, a professor of astronomy at her school, is identical with Danore, Victor's former teacher in England, she loves Victor even more because of Emanuel and calls him the "noble friend of my teacher." In spite of having several love affairs, Victor is not seduced like Gustav, but escapes at the very last moment. Klotilde seems to be more reasonable than Beata. Aside from a mystical love for her dead companion Giulia, she moves serenely and reasonably through the dangerous intrigues at the court, where she lives as maid of honor to the prince's young wife, with whom Victor is also in love. When he learns that he is not Lord Horion's son but the minister's offspring, he no longer considers himself to be Klotilde's match and is willing to renounce her. But she does not hesitate to marry a commoner.

Hans Bach enumerates twenty-five points of comparison between *Hesperus* and *The Invisible Lodge*.[67] I will discuss only two of them: the political theme and the role of the storyteller. In Lord Horion, Jean Paul created the farseeing politician, whose only goal is the welfare of the state. He is responsible for the kidnapping of the prince's sons and directs their education in England. He also plans to present them to their father when they are ready to become his counselors and replace the evil advisers surrounding the throne. When he is no longer needed, he commits suicide by the grave of his wife, where he hopes to rest in peace. Jean Paul's revolutionary ideas were strengthened by the progress of the French Revolution. He began to write

Hesperus in 1792, the year of the assault on the Tuileries; and in 1793, when Louis XVI was decapitated, he had not yet finished the novel. During Robespierre's government, he wrote to his friend Otto that it was impertinent of princes to commit injustices and acts of folly at the same time. In such cases, they would only be shaken from their thrones like apples from a tree.[68]

In his novel, Jean Paul is more reserved in his political pronouncements. The revolutionary "Englishmen" who blow up the powder magazine are the extremists, whereas Victor, the true democrat, tries to follow a more moderate path. He maintains that a free state is not a warrant for lower taxes, more luxurious living, greater security of property, in short, for an increase of material goods, all of which can exist in monarchies as well. If we are willing to sacrifice our property and lives in the fight for freedom, we should have higher goals than life and property. The strictest despot ensures his subjects' physical and material prosperity for egotistical reasons. Like his contemporaries, Jean Paul believed in cosmopolitanism. He did not share, however, the hope of the eighteenth century that wars would soon die out. He foresaw long battles, not only within Europe, but between continents: "There still lie four quarters of the globe full of enchained savage races;—their chain daily grows thinner,—time loosens it;—what desolation, at least what changes, must they not bring about on the little bowling-green of our cultivated countries?"[69]

According to Jean Paul, the root of all evil is inequality in politics and education. In his view, a well-balanced Europe presupposes the equilibrium of the four other continents. Only if all people were wise and good would they be benevolently inclined towards each other.

As that is not so, accordingly Nature makes up for this goodness by similarity of motives, by community of object, by living together, etc., and by these bonds—of connubial, or brotherly and sisterly and of friendly affection—holds our smooth, slippery hearts together at different distances. Thus she educates our hearts to the higher warmth. The State gives it a still greater, for the citizen loves the man even more in the citizen, than the brother loves him in the brother, the father in the son. The love of country is nothing but a restricted cosmopolitan love; and the higher philanthropy is the philosopher's enlarged patriotism for the whole earth.[70]

Jean Paul's treatment of the storyteller in this novel is superb. The biographer or chronicler Jean Paul lives on an island, where he is regularly visited by a Pomeranian dog carrying around his neck a cask carved out of a pumpkin, which contains reports signed by Knef. The illusion is created that the chronicler does not know any more than does the reader, both of whom depend on the contents of the cask. Knef, the inversion of "Fenk," lives with Victor as his servant in order to get first-hand information on Victor, the court, and the "Englishmen," for the Lord. When the chronicler goes on a trip to visit his friend Christian Otto, he is suddenly attacked and taken to the island of Reunion. There he learns that he is the fifth son of the prince, called "Mosge," meaning Monsieur, the title given to the brother of the French king. With this trick the storyteller vanishes before the reader's eyes into the story.[71] In the beginning, the plot of the novel and the chronicler's biography are shown as separate tracks, but they are interwoven shortly before the end, combining a Sterne-like caprice and the traditional auctorial novel. With this synthesis, Jean Paul created a new form of the novel, leading *ad absurdum* the skepticism against the novel in general.[72] The presentation of the two worlds, fiction and reality, allows the reader to slip from one to the other, to slide from thinking to feeling, from humor to ecstasy,[73] and to get full benefit of Jean Paul's complex of contrasts and dissonances, which causes "despair to the naïve reader and delight to higher spirits."[74] As Jean Paul said, he did not write for a "Minorität" but for a "Minimität."[75]

CHAPTER 4

Titan

I The Plot

WHEREAS *Wutz* and *Siebenkäs* have gained a certain popularity among educated German readers, Jean Paul's masterpiece, *Titan,* is still considered a difficult novel with a plot nobody understands. But in Emil Staiger's view *Titan* "opens itself up most easily"[1] to the modern reader. My experience is based on the reaction of students in a graduate class who were enthusiastic about Jean Paul's idylls, *Siebenkäs* and the *Flegeljahre,* but incapable of finishing *Titan.* People who have read Goethe's *Wilhelm Meister* several times, and even Wieland's *Agathon* from cover to cover, who rave about Wolfram's *Parzival* and love and admire Keller's *Green Henry,* fall asleep, or into despair, when they try to read the first of the four volumes of this work. However, if they are able to take this first hurdle, they are likely to finish the novel with growing interest, appreciation, and delight. What is the reason for this initial difficulty?

It is true that the plot of *Titan* is confusing. Jean Paul himself admitted that it was almost impossible for him simply to tell a story. For him the characters represented, in one way or other, the essential ideas of the novel or else himself, and were thus the germ cell of his work.[2] He had not quite laid out a plan for the novel as a whole when he was already writing the second volume. The plot finally emerged to take its course as follows: The hero of the novel, Albano, is shown in his physical and mental development from early childhood to maturity. He does not know that he is the younger brother of the crown prince of Hohenfliess but believes the knight Gaspard to be his father. Gaspard's wife, the Princess di Lauria, had given birth to a little girl, Linda, at almost the same time at which the Princess of Hohenfliess gave birth to the twins Albano and Julienne. Nobody knew about Albano's birth for he was taken immediately and secretly to Isola Bella in Lago Maggiore, where he was brought up with Linda, whose mother was the best friend of Albano's mother. The parents of the two children knew that they had to protect the little prince against the conspiracy of the ruling prince of Haarhaar, who was waiting rather impatiently for the extinction of the dynasty of Hohenfliess, because he wanted to join both realms under his scepter. In order to hasten this process, the prince's most obedient servant, Monsieur de Bouverot, had induced Albano's older brother Luigi, the crown prince, to lead the life of a debauchee in Rome, which ruined him completely as a man and as a leader.

Albano, on the other hand, led a protected life as Gaspard's son, first in Italy, and later on in Blumenbühl near Pestitz, the capital of Hohenfliess. In the house of the director of landscaping, Wehrfritz, he received all the warmth a child needs from Wehrfritz himself, his wife Albine, and their daughter Rabette. Linda, who had been taken to Spain after her mother's death, was passed off for Gaspard's foster daughter. Before his marriage, Gaspard had unsuccessfully sought the hand of the princess of Haarhaar. His only goal was now to have at least his daughter Linda married to Albano, so that his grandchildren would have the advantage of being members of a ruling dynasty, an advantage that he had been denied. For this reason, he separated Linda and Albano while they were still children, so that they should meet again at the prime of their age and fall in love. Gaspard prepares them for that moment with an elaborate machinery of tricks, illusions, and voices out of the air (Gaspard's brother is a ventriloquist and is used by him for his purposes). On one occasion, Linda's head (really a wax bust) emerges from Lago Maggiore, and words from nowhere accompany the apparition: "Love the beautiful one, I shall help you to win her!" Albano is disgusted with this jugglery, but he cannot help being in some way impressed by it.

Since his early youth, Albano has been in love with a girl he has never seen—Liane von Froulay, the daughter of the prime minister of Hohenfliess. Liane's brother, Roquairol, seems to him an ideal friend, although he has never met him. But their common teacher for dancing and fencing has told him so much about brother and sister that, in his imagination, they are closest to his heart.

Until his twentieth birthday, Albano is not permitted to go to Pestitz, the capital of his future realm, because the people might recognize him as the old prince's son, as long as the father is not changed by old age. When Albano finally returns to Pestitz, the old prince and his wife, Albano's mother, have just died.

At the age of twelve, Roquairol had met Linda at a fancy-dress ball where he was dressed as Werther and she as Lotte. Naturally, he fell in love with her, since she was beautiful and brilliant. But when she did not listen to his declaration of love, he shot himself with a pistol, wounding himself in the ear—a deed for which Albano admired him extravagantly. Many years later, when the two young men meet for the first time, Albano swears that he will never strive for Linda's love, since he is in love with Liane, whose name he does not mention. Albano and Roquairol become ardent friends.

Happy weeks follow their first meeting in Blumenbühl, where Liane lives as a guest in Wehrfritz's house. Roquairol is enchanted by Rabette's naïveté, and the two happy couples do not think that there could be any obstacle to their love. But this idyll runs against Gaspard's plans. Liane is secretly told of Albano's noble birth, which forbids her to pursue her happiness. She renounces him without telling the reason, and he leaves her angrily. Heartbroken, she loses her eyesight and dies without giving the secret of Albano's noble birth away. Now Albano breaks down, overwhelmed by guilt feelings. In that critical moment, his teacher and friend Schoppe brings Idoine, princess of Haarhaar, into Albano's room. Albano thinks it is Liane, because the two young girls look very much alike. Idoine, playing the role of Liane, forgives Albano his deadly suspicion. He regains his health but loses his friend Roquairol, who tells him in a letter that he has seduced Rabette and left her for good.

Albano is taken to Rome, where he is less interested in art than in the grandeur of the city's past, which inspires him to active life. He plans to fight *in tyrannos* for France's freedom during the Great Revolution. In Ischia he meets his twin sister Julienne as well as Linda, who appears to be his match in appearance, intellect, and soul. Gaspard believes that his highest ambition has been realized; for Linda and Albano are an ideal couple.

After their return to Pestitz, however, Gaspard's plans are thwarted by Linda's independence and Roquairol's viciousness. Linda wants to give herself to Albano without bourgeois-like ties, only obeying her passion. Roquairol takes advantage of her night-blindness and the similarity of his voice to Albano's. In the same park in which Albano and Roquairol had sworn eternal friend-ship, Roquairol seduces Linda, who thinks that she is holding Albano in her arms. The next evening, Roquairol plays the last act of his life on a stage in the park, killing himself at the end of the play. Linda calls herself Roquairol's widow and leaves with Gaspard. At Liane's grave, Albano meets Liane's double, Idoine. It seems to him that he has always loved Idoine, without being aware of it. She is an active, intelligent young woman, who is deeply interested in her subjects' welfare. And she has created a model estate for them, a near-Paradise, where they must work hard but enjoy life. Luigi, Albano's older brother, finally dies, and there are no more obstacles to Albano's ascend-ing the throne. He marries Idoine, thereby uniting the two prin-cipalities.

II Confusing Factors

A The Engagement of the Imagination

There is no doubt that this confusing story would hardly in-duce anybody to struggle through four volumes written in a highly complex style. Nevertheless, there must be some value attached to this novel, which Jean Paul considered his master-piece. At least he affirmed in 1805 that he himself could not sur-pass the last two volumes.[3] His contemporaries, who had been so enthusiastic about his earlier novels, *The Invisible Lodge* and *Hesperus*, were uneasy about *Titan*. Even Jean Paul's best friends hesitated to make their reactions known, although he urged them to criticize the work quite frankly.

Among the celebrities of his time, Wieland alone was deeply moved by the novel. After having read the eighth chapter, in which Albano, Liane, a sixteen-year-old Greek mother, and her little girl walk through a serene park full of fountains, and through a valley where flutes play automatically, Wieland praised Jean Paul as an almost divine creator of the most sublime, deli-cate, idealistic and, at the same time, purely human beings.[4]

Posterity has been of two minds. If we take Stefan George's interpretation, which considers only scenes with a sentimental climax—like dreams, prayers, letters, first encounters, thunderstorms, farewells, and deaths—we must unrestrainedly admire Jean Paul's achievement of the purest poetry. Twelve years after Stefan George's eulogy, Wilhelm Scherer maintained that Jean Paul's readers had repeatedly rejected his novels because of the author's inability to create credible characters, abnormal people being presented with virtuosity, but grotesque exaggeration, and normal people remaining vague, unreal, and unbelievable. Scherer also reproached Jean Paul with his lack of form, and with the overabundance of far-fetched metaphors, abstruse comparisons, awkward sentences, and superfluous footnotes.[5] All of this, apparently, prevented Jean Paul from presenting his profound ideas in a readable form and from shaping them into a masterpiece.

Jean Paul himself refuted Scherer more than a hundred years in advance. In his *Comic Appendix to Titan* (1800–1801), he defended his novel by referring its critics to Mozart's *Magic Flute*, where the audience has to enjoy concurrently the "chaos of all the instruments, all the actors, their visual pantomime and exotic sound effects, the fantastic play itself and, finally, the splendor of the decoration."[6] All this, he felt, was more demanding than the reading of his novel. Emil Staiger also compares *Titan* to an opera, but for another reason. He maintains that the text does not have to have literary value as long as it gives the composer an opportunity to produce good music.

But where is the good music in the novel? Is any of it inspired by the plot, which is as cumbersome and painful as everything in this world that imprisons our soul? Jean Paul, after all, wanted to free the soul, to open a window on eternity, which he believed was visible to the human mind. The way to eternity, as Staiger points out, is for Jean Paul the removal of substance. Toward this end he sets everything in motion. Nothing is static, and the present moment has value only insofar as it is filled with memory of the past and insight into the future. Thus the power that enables a human being to seek and reach eternity is that of the imagination.[7]

Jean Paul expresses this idea even more emphatically by stating: "Only the paradise of the imagination willingly remains and is never lost, but always conquered. Poetry alone reconciles the past to the future, and is the Orpheus lyre which commands these two destroying rocks to rest. [Footnote by Jean Paul]: It is well known that the Simplegadian rocks continually dashed against each other, and destroyed every passing ship, until Orpheus' lyre subdued and tranquillized them." [8]

The imagery in the *Titan* engages our imagination. Thus with the help of this magic power, Pestitz (the city which Albano is not allowed to enter but can see from a distance) becomes for him, as for us, a miráculous place we approach with trepidation. Verbs of motion like point, spur, fly up, stretch down, blaze far and wide, direct towards, run, turn towards, stretch out, graze, jog along, float, call together, hammer away, clatter around, keep us engaged, so that we are ready, like Albano, to experience past and future within a single moment:

When he came back to the fork of the road, of which the right prong points to Lilar, Albano, with a somewhat heavy heart, spurred his horse across, and flew up the hill, till the bright city, like an illuminated St. Peter's dome, blazed far and wide in this spring night of fancies. . . . The long wall of the palaces of the mountain-city gleamed from above a welcome to our Albano, and the statues, on their Italian roofs, directed themselves towards him as way-guides and criers of joy; over all the palaces ran the iron framework of the lightning-rods, like a throne-scaffolding of the thunder, with golden scepter-points. . . carpenters were hammering away, children were clattering around with the birchbark; cloth-makers were stretching out green cloths like bird-nets in the sun; from the distance came white-covered carriers' wagons jogging along the country-road, and by the sides of the way shorn sheep were grazing under the warm shadow of the rich, bright linden-blossoms. [9]

The effect of motion is even stronger when Albano himself is caught in it on the spiral alleys leading to the top of the hill.

The foliage, with its spiral alleys, wound him round into a deeper and deeper night, through which not the moon, but only the heat lightning, with which the warm, cloudless heavens were overcharged, could break. The magic circles of the mount rose ever smaller and smaller out of the leaves into the blossoms . . . he climbed amid summits and roots behind the aromatic balustrade toward heaven; but the little spiral alley running round with him hung before the stars purple night-violets and hid the deeper garden with orange summits; at length he sprang from the highest rung of his Jacob's ladder, with all his senses, out into an uncovered, living heaven; a

light hilltop, only fringed with variegated flowercups, received him
and cradled him under the stars. . . . (I, 140)

Albano's love for Liane and Roquairol long before he meets
them, is another product of Jean Paul's rich imagination. Liane
herself is more real in his dreams than in real life, since his love
for her is ecstasy. She could never join the ranks of characters,
created by great authors, that have gained a new reality for us,
like Hamlet, Faust, Don Quixote, and Achilles. Liane is moving
toward death in the same way that Jean Paul's settings move
toward dissolution into impressionistic color schemes, music, and
atmosphere ("Stimmung").

In an easy chair lay a white-clad figure, with pale sunken cheeks . . .
leaning her head, which was encircled with a variegated wreath of
wild flowers, on the arm of the chair. It was his former Liane . . .
she said with a heavy smile: "So, then, thou lovest me again, Albano
. . . farewell, beloved . . . je ne suis qu'un songe . . . ." Liane grew
paler and paler; death arrayed her in the white bridal-garment of
Heaven. . . . Pale and glorified with the moonlight of the higher
world was the strange form which passed majestically forth from
the midst of puny living among its lofty dead. Then gushed the
golden sun through the clouds . . . and circumfused with the blooming evening twilight the faded sister of heaven . . . all the clouds,
touched with her wings as she swept through them, burst out into
long, red blossoms. . . .

The twentieth-century reader must overcome his embarrassment in the presence of these "titanic" characters and their overwhelming feelings. He prefers not to be constantly directed into
metaphysics but would rather "stay in the nest, deaf-blind, in
an animal presence." [10] Besides, he is used to hiding his feelings
or expressing them in a more subdued fashion. It is no longer
considered good manners to show strong emotions, and tears are
not shed in public. This was different at the beginning of the
nineteenth century during the period of "Empfindsamkeit." To
read about the friendship between two young men like Albano
and Roquairol, who kiss and embrace each other (a natural gesture in Jean Paul's times), is upsetting, and Albano's adoration
of Liane, whom he considers a saint, seems exaggerated. He
kisses her as the apostle John kissed Jesus. Staiger points out
that with this comparison even the difference of sex is nullified.[11]

B *Similarity of Characters*

Another confusing factor for the present-day reader is the basic similarity of certain pairs of principal characters who seem, indeed, to be very different at first glance. Emil Staiger explains this phenomenon by showing that Albano and Roquairol, like Walt and Vult in *The Twins*, are actually manifestations of Jean Paul himself. He quotes Jean Paul, who attempts to prove in a "massive" way that the difference between the two protagonists is based on their religious attitude: Albano, the idealist, believes in God, whereas Roquairol, the enlightened realist, does not. But does Albano really believe in an objective power independent of himself? Does anything exist that has not been created by him?[12]

Although knowing better, Jean Paul liked to interpret Fichte's absolute ego as the empiric ego, and presents the characters in the novel as Solipsists who believe that everything in this world is created by themselves since the world is nothing but a mental image, a conception of the individual. These titanic egos end as cynics and go to pieces in their loneliness.

At the end of the novel Albano sums up his life in the following manner: "A voice spoke within him: 'What has there been then? . . . What is left? A wide woe over the whole heart; but the heart too remains—empty, of course, but firm, sound, hot . . . I still wish; I still want . . . what has gone down will come again and flee again, and only that will remain true to thee which is forsaken—thyself alone.'"[13] In a letter which Staiger calls "devilish," Roquairol predicts that Albano will become more and more like Roquairol himself.

As thou so readily assumest every difference from thyself to be enervation, so do I say to thee outright: Only ascend farther, only knead yourself more thoroughly, only lift thy head higher out of the hot waves of the feelings, then wilt thou no longer lose thyself in them, but let them billow alone. There is a cold daring spirit in man which nothing touches at all, not even virtue, for it alone chooses that and is its creator, not its creature. I once experienced a storm at sea, in which all the elements, furious and rough and foaming, lashed themselves into commotion and flung their waters pell-mell against each other, while overhead the sun looked on in silence—so be thou! The heart is the storm, self is the heaven.[14]

A third incarnation of Jean Paul, his most favorite character in the novel, is Schoppe, Albano's adviser and friend. He is shaped after Swift's model, as the realist-humorist who does not try to dissolve reality in order to reach eternity with the help of the magic imagination, but focuses instead on near objects in the real world, realizing that everything is wrong and that the world's ills are incurable. This knowledge does not disappoint him because he did not expect anything better. Like Albano and Roquairol, he suffers from another vital imperfection, absolute loneliness.

I am surrounded by humanity turned into stone—in the dark uninhabited silence there glows no love, no admiration, no prayer, no hope, no goal—I am totally alone, no pulse, no life, nothing around me, and nothing without me, but nothing—I am only conscious of my higher non-consciousness—within me the mute, blind demogorgon, working in disguise, and I am he himself ([footnote] Gorgo changes into stone whoever looks into her face; demo = daemon.)— thus I come from eternity, thus I go to eternity—and who hears my complaint and knows me now?—I—who hears it and who knows me after eternity?—I.—[15]

In his *Introduction to Esthetics*, Jean Paul explains how a character should be introduced to the reader by a gradual "unveiling," revealing his appearance and his soul through action and emotion.[16] We are shown Liane for the first time when Albano visits her parents. He stands at the window of Liane's room and sees her hidden by a circle of jets of water. This is a cure suggested by her doctor, who thinks that high humidity will heal Liane's nervous blindness. The water is hit by moonlight, so that Albano can hardly see more than a figure in white in an impressionistic composition of light and silvery water. The next day, when Albano secretly enters the garden and approaches the edge of the fountain in order to see Liane from nearby, the water is shut off. Like a curtain, disappearing in the ground, the half-transparent wall of water is taken away and "unveils" Liane to Albano, who is moved by her beauty and delicate dignity.

Albano, the protagonist of the novel, is "unveiled" in the very first chapter when he is taken by boat to Isola Bella in Lago Maggiore. He closes his eyes while his friends describe to him the beauty of the scenery—a beauty and perfection he does not want to spoil by a gradual approach. He prefers, instead, a single moment of total rapture. The reader understands that this very young man, whom we might call high-strung and whom Jean Paul calls titanic, i.e., unbalanced, inharmonious, chaotic, will have to calm down before he can act intelligently and effectively. Right at the beginning, we grasp the first theme of the novel, the transformation of the young Titan into a being who lives in harmony with himself and his environment. When these Titans —all the main characters belong to this group—are incapable of fulfilling this condition, they will come to grief, be it death, suicide, or loss of love or happiness. Liane is a Titan of feeling and emotion; Roquairol is the unrestrained actor and author of his own life, always performing on a real or imaginary stage; Gaspard is the egotistic pursuer of his ends, using human beings as tools in his well-planned schemes; Schoppe is the one-sided philosopher who, misguided by Fichte's idealism, loses contact with man and reality and, finally, with himself. The fate of these characters develops from their essential nature with the necessity of Greek tragedy. In both cases, we witness the destruction of titanic characters in their encounter with a metaphysical power.

The second volume of the *Comic Appendix* contains the *Logbook of the Balloonist Giannozzo*. Giannozzo is an intensification of Schoppe, a character who increasingly captures the interest of the modern reader. He is the purest incarnation of Jean Paul's "humorists," like Leibgeber in *Siebenkäs* and Vult in *The Twins*. All contrasts are comprised in Giannozzo; he is the wise fool and belongs to two worlds; for although he is a part of our world, he looks down on us from the heights of the satiric and universal humorist who measures the infinite with finiteness. This kind of humor, which can only grow out of a tragic philosophy of life, frees Giannozzo from mankind and from himself.[17]

He lives in the comfortably furnished nacelle of his balloon. The nacelle is shaped like a die, with windows on all six sides that allow him to look down on the earth from such a distance that it appears to him like a spittoon, in Dutch "quispedoor,"[18] purposely changed by Jean Paul to "Pissbidorchen," and thus stating in one syllable, the first one, Giannozzo's humorous "evaluation" of the earth. He calls the nacelle his "Siechkobel," alluding to the tiny hut outside the city walls, where, during the

Middle Ages, people with incurable contagious diseases lived as outcasts. A "Siechkobel" is the perfect symbol for the home of a person who despises mankind and leads a life apart from others because he suffers from being exposed to their stupidity and cruelty.

Floating in the ether gives moments of exalted happiness to Giannozzo, but he has moments when confronted with nothingness of despair as well. He then descends as a visitor to this world looking for company which, however, he cannot stand for more than a moment. He loves beautiful scenery, but only when seen from above; he admires and kisses a young woman who is waiting for her lover, and finally helps to bring the two together. But he loses all self-control as he watches soldiers fighting on a battlefield. In his anger, he drops all the rocks which constitute his ballast. He consequently not only participates in the battle, killing men with his rocks, but exposes himself to a thunderstorm, which he cannot escape because, by not having any ballast left, he cannot rise above it. Since there is no way out, he blows a little horn, the metal of which attracts the lightning, and thus perishes, the lower part of his face torn off by the lightning bolt.

During his escape from this world, sailing in the sky, Giannozzo never praises the creator but pays his respects to some metaphysical power. He even feels a slight hope for himself when he asks himself, during a sunset, whether he, too, might rise one day into another world. This question is not asked at the end of the story, Giannozzo's fourteenth trip, but during the eleventh one. The conclusion of the story depicts nothing but the triumphant self-destruction and the horrifying naturalistic description of Giannozzo's mutilated face. Involuntarily, the reader thinks of the end of Faust in the chapbook where Faust's disciples find his limbs scattered all over the yard. Giannozzo's friend finds the corpse and the logbook, which will be read by all those who feel like Giannozzo, so that they may have the courage—or listen to the warning—to lead or not to lead a life similar to his and end like him: proud, independent, but destroyed by their own extravagance.

Kommerell interprets *Titan* as a discussion of the spiritual struggles of the age. In Weimar and in Berlin, Jean Paul met the giants of Neo-Classicism and Romanticism, who were able to exist without the help of belief in a metaphysical power, and who considered themselves to be as independent and powerful as gods. Jean Paul symbolically represented his own struggle and that of his contemporaries, and thus he became a judge and interpreter of his time.[19]

III *Stylistic Devices*

A *Figures of Speech*

Jean Paul's reader is never permitted to sit back and be entertained, nor can he be content with being receptive, because the author forces him by various stylistic devices to participate, actively and even creatively. Jean Paul attains this result merely by jolting the imagination; and his most convincing device, he felt, was the visual image, the direct presentation of figures and actions or the sharp visual metaphor. He felt that the visual image activates the poetic imagination more strongly than its aural counterpart.

Knowing this aspect of his esthetic, we are not surprised by his extensive use of visual metaphor, which he requires to be novel and sensually beautiful in order to be perfect. Detailed studies on the use of the metaphor in Jean Paul's works have been made, and more will be produced, because in form and content his imagery is inexhaustibly rich.[20] In this monograph it is sufficient to give some examples to engage *our* reader's imagination.

If a figure of speech is handled like a musical theme with all its variations and modulations, Jean Paul calls it an allegory. He warns authors against such a form because there is the danger of mixing or confusing metaphors instead of subtly varying them. He quotes one example from Lessing, which shows that even a good writer can produce a poor allegory.

I unroll the cocoon of silkworms, not to teach the silkworms how to spin (this sounds already as if one wrote: I shear the sheep, but not to teach them how to wear wool—), but rather to make purses from that silk, purses for me and people like me (—why purses and not socks, etc., and if purses, why made of silk?—); purses, to go on with the simile (rather an allegory), into which I'll collect the small coins of individual sensations (—where is the natural transition from silkworm to coins, which runs into a third allegory because the coins are *small*), until I can exchange them into the good valuable goldpieces of general remarks (—very clumsy indeed; does he hope to get ahead with the help of *good, valuable, gold?*—) and add them to the capital of self-thought truths (—here I see the fourth allegory, but what happened to the silkworms?—) [21]

Jean Paul himself, writing allegorically on the allegory, does not do it too well either, as he himself readily admits. He discusses, for instance, the style of Klopstock "who stops in front of an ordinary metaphorical flower and pulls apart its leaves and stamens to an allegory and dusts with its pollens the following sentences." [22] However, in his novel he is a master of this figure of speech, e.g., when he describes Albano's "transplantation" from Italy to Germany:

After the death of his mother his father transplanted him from the garden-mould of Italy—some of which, however, still adhered to the tap-roots—into the royal forest of Germany . . . ; there he had him educated in the house of a worthy nobleman, or to speak more pithily, significantly, and allegorically, he caused the pedagogical professional gardeners to run round him with their water-pots, grafting-knives, and pruning-shears, till the tall, slender palm-tree, full of sagopith and protecting thorns, outgrew them, and could no longer be reached by their pots and shears.

And now, when he shall have returned from the island, he is to pass from the field-bed of the country to the tan-vat and hot-bed of the city, and to the trellises of the court garden; in a word, to Pestitz. . . .[23]

Jean Paul prefers the simile to the allegory, calling it "more valuable and more difficult than one hundred allegories." [24] "Wit . . . sees the relationships of similarities, i.e., partial likeness, hidden under greater difference; sagacity sees the relationships of dissimilarities, i.e., partial difference, hidden under greater likeness; profundity sees complete likeness in spite of the (misleading) appearance." [25]

A comparison must be short, must concentrate on the main points and eliminate all dissimilar minor points: ([footnote] "Brevity is the body and the soul of wit. . . . People always hope (in the reader's semi-sleep) to have grasped in advance the minor proposition while reading the major proposition, so that they can pleasantly use for recreation the time which is spent reading the minor one—but how startled they are (and this gives them strength) when they see that they did not guess a thing in advance, and that they have to think again and again from one comma to the next comma . . ." (p. 162).

A good comparison forces the intellect quickly to run through a thought pattern twice, for instance: "Formerly, in ancient Rome, temples preserved libraries; nowadays libraries preserve temples (because nowadays divine service is held mostly by reading a good book)" (I, 163). Our intellect is kept busy with unmetaphorical comparisons, whose roots do not contain figurative similarities. It is our imagination that is stimulated by metaphorical comparisons. However, it is easier to represent a particular than to concretize an abstraction, because it comes more easily to us to say "The high wind is angry" than "Wrath is a gale." Jean Paul devotes a long chapter to the discussion of the different kinds of comparisons, thus showing how important this figure of speech was to him. But the reader can enjoy his imagery thoroughly without having studied in detail the *Introduction to Esthetics*.

Jean Paul himself furnishes us with the purest example of the plain witty comparison in describing the effect of favorable criticism: "I will hold the magic leaf of a favorable criticism before a gnashing were wolf: immediately he will stand before me like a licking lamb, with little twirling tail" (I, 98).

Equally witty is the description of the suffering of a poor teacher attending a gala dinner: "Wehmeier, to tell the truth, had the greatest reluctance to eat with a nobleman, merely because, as entertaining *acteur* of the table, he had so much to do with conversing, *savoir-vivre*, looking out for others, keeping his limbs in proper attitude, and passing all eatables, that, for want of leisure, he was obliged to swallow such little things as pickled cucumbers, chestnuts, crabs' tails, and the like, down whole, and without tasting them; so that afterward he often had to carry round with him the hard fodder, like a swallowed Jonah, for three days together in the hunter's pouch of his stomach" (I, 98–99). A good exercise for the intellect is the description of the financial straits of Albano's dancing instructor: "The poor devil was to be sure poor and believed, with many other authors that unlike Solomon, who prayed for wisdom and had received gold, he had conversely had the misfortune while supplicating for the latter to receive only the former" (I, 124). Occasionally

Jean Paul uses learned comparisons that require a complete
synthesis of knowledge, thinking and combinatory power. Thus
Albano learns that Liane is seriously ill and that her mother
fears for her life. He has not yet met Liane, but he has read
two little notes from her in a calendar which he borrowed from
her mother's library through their teacher. On the two last pages
of thick vellum Liane had written, "Concert for the Poor, February 21; Play for the Poor, November 1st." All this we must
remember when we read in the next chapter: "And then this
Philomela without a tongue, because she had hitherto been
compelled to be dumb, had, like Procne, sent him only the pic-
tured history of her hearty existence, and only the leaves of
Parchment" (I, 133).

The reader who is well versed in Greek mythology knows that
Philomela and Procne are sisters. Procne's husband Tereus rav-
ishes Philomela and tears out her tongue, so that she cannot
reveal his misdeed. She embroiders her story with scarlet thread
on a white gown, which she sends to her sister. Procne and Philomela kill Tereus's son Itys. Tereus persecutes them, and eventually all three of them are changed into birds—Philomela into a
nightingale, Procne into a lark, and Tereus into a hoopoe. Most
readers are familiar with the metamorphosis of Philomela, but
they forget the rest of the myth and have to reread it before
they can understand Jean Paul's allusion. Thus they are likely
to blame him for being so "difficult" instead of blaming their
readers are familiar with the metamorphosis of Philomele, but
own faulty recollection.

Whereas the author and the lamb of the first simile, the un-
digested food and Jonah, Liane and the ravished Philomela are
truly dissimilar and only joined with the help of the predicate,
which is typical for unmetaphorical comparisons, Jean Paul
stimulates our imagination with the following metaphor. When
Albano is informed about his mother's "testamentary whirl and
whiz," he is not affected, except that it produces "a more tender
love for his good mother who, when she already beheld, in the
stream of life below, the swift image of the pouncing hawk of
death, thought only of her son" (I, 36).

His confirmation takes place on Whitsunday, during a thunderstorm: "Early in the morning the dark powderhouse of a storm
cloud stood mute near the hot sun, and was glowing with his
beams; and only occasionally, during divine service, some strange

distant cloud let fall a clap on the fire-drum" (I, 136). The thunderstorm rages and wears out before the end of the service. Albano steps out of the church, "and the glistening sun looked down with a friendly smile on the affrighted earth, whose bright tears still quivered in all her flower-eyes. . . . By the soft dead-gold of resting fancy, and by the holy stillness of the regenerated bosom, and by the increased fervor of his love, there grew up out of all regions of his soul an evening-red, magic Arcadia . . . " (I, 137–38).

Around that time, Albano's mother and sister, unknown to him, visit his foster-parents. After the visit all members of the family are "eager to say three words upon the lavender-water of joy, that leaves such a fragrance behind it . . ." (I, 148). Albano's studies also provide him with "wings for every Mount Tabor" (I, 156).

Liane's father oppresses his daughter with his unbending character: "The hard strata of such connections as those through which Liane's life-rill must needs filter and force its way, make it purer and clearer, just as all hard strata are filtering stones of water—and all her charms indeed become through her father's tyranny, torments, but also all her torments become, through her own patience, charms" (I, 126).

Inspired by his studies of Greek literature and philosophy, Albano writes his first paper, an exercise considered most important by Jean Paul. According to him, a man may read thirty years and gain less insight than he would gain by writing for six months:

In the beginning, and on the very threshold of the essay perhaps, Albano still crept along step by step and made use merely of his head; but as he got further on and his heart quivered with wings, and like a comet he must needs sweep along before only shimmering constellations of great truths, could he then restrain himself from imitating the rosy-red Flamingo, who in his passage towards the sun, seems to paint himself into a flying brand and to clothe himself in wings of fire? (I, 152-53).

Our discussion of metaphor and simile should be followed by a word on the most popular figure of speech, the pun. Since Aristotle and Cicero the play on words has been widely popular and admired; only the eighteenth century had banned it. Jean Paul was naturally in favor of puns because he liked to play with images and words and felt that such play gave him spiritual freedom. However he was not unaware of the dangers of the exaggerated use of puns:

I shall not conceal one danger from players upon words who want to be nothing else but players. They might get too much used to the temptations of the restricted ear and forget about the far-seeing eye. The pun turns our eyes too easily from large and wide objects to particles of particles. . . . In poetry (as in nature) only the whole is the father of the great-grandsons; but single tiny taylor-birds, the particles, will never become fathers of eagles.[26]

Most puns are untranslatable because they are based on the double meaning of a word. Here is one sentence with four puns referring to Roquairol's attempted suicide and to Falterle's, the music and dancing instructor's, shyness: "For the inventively rich Roquairol had with that shot at himself in his thirteenth year saluted and won the whole female sex, and turned himself from a sacrificial victim into the priest of sacrifices and manager of the amateuress-theatre, attached to the amateur-theatre; whereas the shy, stupid Falterle, with his still-born fancy, could never bring a charmer to any other step than the *pas retrograde* in a minuet, or to anything more than a setting of the fingers, when he wanted himself set in the heart" (I, 119–120).

Wit stands in high esteem with Jean Paul because "freedom gives wit and wit gives freedom." Children should be trained in the use of wit, and old people should allow wit to liberate them from the burden of proof. "Wit, the anagram of nature, denies ghosts and gods; it is part of no being, only of its relations; it neither respects nor denies; everything is equal for wit . . . wit plays for the sake of playing."[27]

Since the Germans lack nothing but freedom for wit, they should allow themselves this freedom.[28] Jean Paul himself does not need this advice because freedom is the fundamental premise of his life and work. Metaphors, allegories, similes, puns, all arise from the free play of wit and from the juxtaposition of dissimilarities. Jean Paul's play of wit for the sake of playing deserves one last example: "Every young man has a fine season in his life when he will accept no office, and every young woman has the same in hers, when she will accept no husband; by and by they both change, and often take one another into the bargain" (II, 38–39).

As a master of rhetoric, Jean Paul has at his command all figures of speech. He is the embodiment of all poetics from antiquity through the eighteenth century, as well as of his own poetic *Introduction to Esthetics*. An analytic presentation of the different "flowers of speech" may give the wrong impression of his style, as if he had simply pieced together the different figures. We must do him the justice of considering the following two full paragraphs, one describing Albano's teachers, the other his childhood escape from home. Both descriptions are masterpieces and should not be analyzed, but simply enjoyed. They are not conglomerations of all the particulars mentioned so far, but a complete unit showing irresistible humor in one and humor mixed with emotion in the other.

What a splendidly picturesque contrast of the two brothers-in-office! The master of accomplishments with the motley scarf-skin or hind-apron of a yellow summerdress, as if with the yellow outer wings of a butter-moth, whose dark underwings represent the waistcoat (when he unbuttons it); Wehmeier, on the other hand, in a roomy, sap-green plush, which a tent-maker seemed to have hung on him, and with belly and shanks quivering in the black velvet half-mourning of candidates who wear it till they carbonize into clear black. Falterle had his glazed forest pantaloons plated and cast round his legs, and every wrinkle in them produced one upon his face, as if the latter were the lining of the former; while along the thighs of the Bandbox-master wound upward the cockle-stairs of his swaddling modests. ([footnote]: Some would rather hear this word than breeches.) The former in bridal-shoes, the latter in pump-chambers, the one flapping up like a soft, slimy gold tench with the belly-fins of his bosom-ruffles, with the side-fins of his hand ruffles, and with the tail-fins of a trinomial root or queue hanging on three little ermine tails; the Magister, in his green plush, looking for all the world like a green whiting or a chub. A magnificent set-off, I repeat! (I, 99-100)

Now to Albano's escape. In every word, one feels Jean Paul's love for dogs and his understanding for the boy whose honor was hurt by his foster-father.

A good genius—the yard-dog Melak—had proved the antagonist-muscle and turnpike-gate of the fugitive. That is to say, Melak wanted to go too, and Albano chose rather that a patron and coastguard so serviceable to the castle-yard, and who oftener warned away intruders than the night-watch did themselves, should go home again. Melak was firm in his matters; he wanted reasons—namely, sticks and stones thrown at him; but the weeping boy, whose burning hands the cold nose of the good-natured animal refreshed, could not give him a hard word, but he merely turned the fawning dog right about, and said softly, Go home! But Melak recognized no decrees except loud ones; he kept turning round again; and in the midst of these inversions— during which, in Albano's mind, always on a Brockenberg and seeing giant forms loom and glide through the clouds, his tears and every undeserved word burned deeper and deeper—he was found by his innocent mother. (I, 107-108)

B *Sound and Rhythm*

Jean Paul's prose should be read aloud like poetry. The silent reader misses two important stylistic features, the sound and the rhythm. When Goethe says: "Über allen Gipfeln/Ist Ruh . . . " [Over all the hill-tops/Is rest] his goal is not to describe a forest scene by night, but he conjures up, with the help of sound and rhythm, the impression he experienced that evening and conveys that impression to us as if we had been present.[29]

In discussing **Jean** Paul's rhythm, Kommerell distinguishes two basic rhap**sodic** sentence structures. The first begins with a series of de**pendent** clauses, all of them introduced by the same conjunction. They build up a tension, which finds its resolution in one or several main clauses. The scene described in the following example takes place in the Whitsuntide church during Albano's confirmation. He knows that Liane will take the sacrament in the capital of Hohenfliess at the same hour as he will do so in his small village.

When Albano stepped before the altar with exalted, glorified emotions, and when he ventured only to mask his love for Liane in an inward prayer for her, and in a picture of her today's devotion, and of her pale form in the dark bride-attire of piety, and when he softly felt as if his purified, sanctified soul were now more worthy of that lovely one—just then, the tempest, with all its war machines playing . . . marched over from the city and passed, armed and hot, right over the church. . . . When long flashes blazed about the saints and the angels of the altar, and when the trembling voices of the singers, growing louder, and the tolling of the familiar bells mingled with the crashing thunder, and he caught, amid the deafening din, a high, fine organ-tone, which he took for one of the tones of that unheard harmonica—then he did mount, deified, upon the triumphal thunder-car by the side of his Liane; the theatre-curtain of life and the stage burned away from under him, and they soared away, linked together and radiant, far through the cool, pure ether! (I, 136-37).

The harmonica whose fine tone he mistakenly thinks he has caught is the harmonica which Liane used to play.

The other type of sentence structure uses only main clauses, or parts of them, separated by dashes—all of them coordinated —which results in a marvelous wealth that brings the reader to the point of intoxication. These sentences occur at moments of utmost happiness or despair. Happiness dies away for Albano with an "alarm-cannon: his ambition took arms—his liberty-tree shot forth in blossoms—the standards of his youthful wishes were consecrated and flung to the breeze of heaven—and on the myrtle-crown he covered a heavy helmet with a glittering, high-waving, plumed crest" (I, 130).

In a less martial example of this type, we see Albano on Isola Bella, awakening after a dream in which he has tried in vain to reach a beloved one who dissolved into a tear that sank into his heart:

In a transfiguring, painless death his firm being fluttered loosely around like an uncertain dream—he had been wafted and rocked upward into the starry heaven as on a mother's breast, and all the stars had flowed into the moon and enlarged her glory—his heart, flung into a warm tear, gently dissolved therein—out of him was only shadow, within him dazzling light—the wind of the flying earth swept by before the upright flame of his soul, and it bent not.—Ah, his Psyche glided with keen, unruffled, inaudible falcon-pinions, in silent ecstasy through the thin air of life (I, 50).

Our last example will show Albano at the age of sixteen on the church tower. Here both types of rhapsodic sentence are combined to convey his ecstatic happiness not only through rhythm but also through sound, metaphor, intensely active verbs and adjectives derived from verbs, color, and general suspension of the separation between inner and outer world.

When presently the storm of sound swept and confounded all together, and when the jewel-sparkling of the ponds, and the flowery pleasure-tent of the frolicking spring, and the red castles on the white roads, and the scattered trains of church-going people slowly winding along between the dark-green cornfields, and the stream girdling round the rich pastures and the blue mountains, those smoking altars

of morning sacrifices, and the whole extended splendor of the visible
creation poured into his soul with a glimmering overflow, and all
appeared to him as dim dream-landscape—O then arose his inner
colosseum full of silent godlike forms of spiritual antiques . . . —and
there he saw among the gods a *friend* and a *loved* one reposing, and
he glowed and trembled. . . . Then the bells died away with a heavy
groan, and became dumb—he stepped back from the bright spring
into the dark tower—he fastened his eye only on the empty, blue
night before him into which the distant earth sent up nothing save
sometimes a butterfly blown out of its course, a swallow cruising by
or a pigeon hovering overhead—the blue veil of Ether fluttered in a
thousand folds over veiled gods in the distance—O then, then the
cheated heart could not but exclaim, in its loneliness, Ah! where shall
I find—where, in the wide regions of space, in this short life—the
souls which I love eternally and so profoundly?—Ah, thou dear one!
what is more painfully and longer sought, then, than a heart? When
man stands before the sea and on mountains, and before pyramids
and ruins, and in the presence of misfortune, and feels himself
exalted, then does he stretch out his arms after the great *Friendship*.
—And when music, and moonlight, and spring and spring tears softly
move him, then his heart dissolves, and he wants *Love*. And he who
has never sought either is a thousand times poorer than he who has
lost both. (I, 135-36).

On the basis of the examples taken from *Titan* it seems obvi-
ous that abstract wit and puns as figures of speech are less
poetical than metaphors and similes, because the former, after
all, are unfigurative. The two objects compared are hardly similar; superficially they even seem to be contradictory. Since ancient poetics this figure has been called oxymoron. Through the
inner tension brought about by the contradiction, the reader is
freed from his normal way of thinking. He finds himself floating
in a spiritual atmosphere. The figurative metaphors, on the other
hand, are highly poetical, sentimental, and musical because they
stir up our emotions without bypassing our reason. They overwhelm us by their beauty and profundity. They are truly "Jean-
Paulish" because they allow him to express his vision in words,
a transformation fascinating to all great poets. Jean Paul's only
concern is this rendering of his inner world into language, which
he can best accomplish through an overabundance of imagery,
as is typical of his style. The modern reader who is a follower of
Wolfram von Eschenbach, Johannes Fischart, or Günter Grass,

authors who are also overabundant in their use of metaphor, should be able to appreciate Jean Paul's richness. Only through fantastic imagery can this author convey his message that there is no real difference between outer and inner world: Nature speaks in similes when Man is mute. Kommerell quotes an impressive and enlightening example in which soul becomes reality without an "as if": "When the park proudly became part of the evening sky and entered into their hearts . . . " (p. 62). But such metaphors are rare, even with Jean Paul, because these "lightnings," as he called them, cannot be "made" by the poet but are given to him in a moment of inspiration.

IV *The Narrator; Humor*

The narrator, one of Jean Paul's transfigurations, is ever present. He employs various forms of apostrophe, addresses the reader, gives advice to the protagonist and poses questions. But Jean Paul's narrator does more than interfere occasionally. It sounds like a joke, but it is not, when Kommerell points out that even a simple description of someone drinking a cup of tea is so imbued with characteristic metaphors that Jean Paul or the narrator is present in every word.

Jean Paul was influenced by the English novelists of the eighteenth century, mainly by Fielding, Richardson, and Sterne, his acknowledged models. We are indebted to Victor Lange's enlightening essay "Erzählformen im Roman des 18. Jahrhunderts" [30] for a discussion of the shift, during the eighteenth century, in the relationship of author and narrator, with the former allowing the latter, his fictitious stand-in, to comment on his style and vice versa. Jean Paul takes ample advantage of this function of the invented narrator. In a separate chapter, "Introductory Programme to Titan"— beginning on page 56, so that the reader cannot skip it as easily as he could if it were the preface—he introduces not only the narrator but also invents a collector of source material for Albano's biography, the Privy Legation's Counselor and Feudal Provost of Flachsenfingen, Mr. von Hafenreffer, who is asked to accept the dedication of the novel. All of this is done with tongue in cheek, but from time to time a serious word on esthetics appears suddenly and unexpectedly. Von Hafenreffer declines the dedication because of his purely "mechanical interest" in the beautiful work and suggests that the narrator report only the most indispensable facts. In this humorous way, Jean Paul makes us understand that the history itself is of minor importance. Hafenreffer's letter ends with a Latin line, a cipher that should remain dark for the public, "hic haec hoc hujus huic hunc hac hoc hac hoc." The garbled declension of the demonstrative is not a cipher, but Jean Paul's joke.

In order to appear credible the narrator of *Titan* introduces himself as a character whom we should know from a previous novel, *Hesperus,* where we read in the 45th Dog-Post-Day (the chapters are so called because a dog delivers the parts of the history to the narrator like a postman), that his father is governor of Flachsenfingen. Jean Paul further justifies his narrator's position by making him a law graduate in the code-deciphering department of the Foreign Affairs Chancellery. The corps of ambassadors send him every post-day tons of material in closely sealed packages. They collect it by means of their "legation soothsayers or clairvoyants. . . . Mr. v. Hafenreffer has in every *cul de sac,* servant's chamber and attic, in every chimney and tavern, his opera-glass of a spy, who often, in order to discover one of the hero's virtues, takes upon himself ten sins. . . . Similar biographical Denunciantes and Familiars [are maintained] in several of the German cities . . . in most places one, but in Leipzig two, in Dresden three, in Berlin six, in Vienna as many in every quarter of the city" (I, 62).

The narrator points out that by living at his paternal court he is well equipped to understand the material sent to him because he observes certain sins, like vanity, libertinism, and idleness right under his very eyes. Like Wolfram von Eschenbach, who has fooled philologists with the invention of Kyot, to whom he claims to owe the fable of his *Parzival,* Jean Paul tries to give as much evidence as possible for the existence of his prince of Flachsenfingen. We read, for instance, that the prince considers himself lucky to get his anecdotes from dispatches and not out of his own head. This makes them more probable but, on the other hand, he must decipher them, which is as hard as thinking them out. He threatens and swears that "so soon as one person shall have nosed out the names of the first volumes of *Titan,* disguised as they have been in the best hieroglyphic style of the chancellery offices, [he will] upset his inkstand, and publish no more" (I, 66).

After going to all this trouble to make his narrator credible, Jean Paul proceeds to destroy the effect altogether by becoming serious about his true esthetic goal. The poet "must lend to every historical circumstance which he treats all that is favorable to the poetic illusion as well as keep clear of everything contradictory and . . . he must never sacrifice beauty to truth, but the reverse" (I, 67). Again the reader understands that he is not supposed to expect a "true story" but one that forces him to recreate for himself whatever is important for Jean Paul, and that he will encounter idealized characters and actions rather than realistic ones.

The narrator suggests to the author still another way of plumbing the depths of his theme. Jean Paul is unable to present anybody but himself, an idealized self to be sure; and even the female character is really Jean Paul behind the mask of a beloved woman. He expressly tells us: "The theatrical mask which I have on in my works is not the mask of the Greek comedian, which was embossed after the face of the individual satirized, but the mask of Nero, which, when he acted a goddess on the stage, looked like his mistress, and when he acted a god, like himself" (I, 69). This does not mean that Jean Paul is the only principal character, that *Titan* is a monologue by the narrator, and that a dialogue between him and the reader no longer exists.

In his essay mentioned above Victor Lange shows how the relationship between reader and narrator changed in the course of the eighteenth century. Fielding respected his audience, Richardson selected it, and Sterne neglected it. From this viewpoint, it would seem, on careful analysis, that Jean Paul follows Sterne and Richardson rather than Fielding. Sometimes he neglects the reader altogether and uses "the mighty engines of eloquence" [31] to overwhelm rather than convince and guide him; at other times he seems to feel responsible for his reader, although not in the manner of Fielding, who quoted Cervantes: "I do not, like a *de jure* tyrant, imagine that they are my slaves or my commodity; I am, indeed, set over them for their own good only and was created for their use, and not they for mine." [32] Jean Paul is more inclined to emulate Richardson, who mobilized all his readers' resources and forced them to become involved.

In *Titan* Jean Paul draws a definite line between the monologue of the narrator and the dialogue between narrator and
reader. The narrator organizes and defends the so-called digressions, which are "reduced to prescriptive rights and confirmed in
a servitude. . . . When the tome is ended, then begins . . . a
small one, in which I give just what I choose (only no narrative),
and in which I flit to and fro so joyously, with my long bee's
sting, from one blossom-nectary and honey-cell to another, that
I name the little sub-volume, made up as it is merely for the
private gratification of my own extravagance, very fitly my honeymoon, because I make less honey therein than I eat, busily
employed, not as a working bee to supply the hive, but as a bee-
master to take up the comb" (I, 58). Among these honey-moons,
reprinted as *Comic Appendix to Titan*, the famous *Logbook of
the Balloonist Giannozzo* and the *Clavis Fichtiana*, both far from
being digressions, are rather the heart and soul of the novel.
   Another subtle humorous attack on the suspicious reader who
is afraid of digressions and unwilling to follow the narrator
down paths that may or may not lead to immediate goals comes
in an official announcement of *obbligato leaves* "which admit
absolutely none but pure contemporaneous facts, less immediately connected with my hero, concerning persons, however,
the more immediately connected with him; in the *obbligato
leaves*, moreover, not the smallest satirical extravasate of digression, no, not the size of a blister, is perceptible; but the happy
reader journeys on with his dear ones . . . right through the
ample court-residence . . . amidst purely historical figures,
surrounded on all sides by . . . mounted hordes and companies of
strolling players—and his eye cannot be satisfied with seeing" (I,
58). The first *obbligato leaf*, Cycle 32, is announced after the fact
in Cycle 33. It is a chapter packed full of events: the old prince
dies, his daughter Julienne asks Liane to go with her to Lilar
where the latter's brother, Roquairol, stands as guard at the "bed
of state" of Julienne's father. "While Liane took a longer and
more intense look at the corpse, an ice-cold edge, as if of death's
scythe, cut through her burning brain—the funeral torches (it
seemed to her) burned dimmer and dimmer—then she saw in
the corner of the chamber a dark cloud playing and growing
up—then the cloud began to fly, and, full of gushing night
rushed over her eyes—then the thick night struck deep roots

into her wounded eyes, and the affrighted soul could only say, 'Ah, brother, I am blind!'" (I, 181-83).

Liane is taken home by her friend; she asks the maid to say nothing to her mother who, however, would not end a day without embracing her daughter, and Liane confesses all. A doctor is called, the father storms in and "lets loose several billion-pounders and hand-grenades upon his lady" (I, 184). In a footnote, the reader is informed of the planned divorce of Liane's parents and its deferment because both wish to keep Liane. But the father's love for Liane shows only in his hatred. The chapter ends with the narrator's contemptuous remark: "Out of forbearance, I say nothing further to the old conjugal bully than go—to the devil or at least to bed!" (I, 185).

The use of the musical term *obbligato*, meaning the essential accompaniment to the principal voice, is apt; for Albano is not mentioned, but the people close to him, like Liane and Roquairol, are described in detail. There is no satirical digression, and this is certainly a chapter that can be enjoyed by the most casual reader, without his even being aware of the masterful description of approaching blindness, which is in Jean Paul's best musical prose. But twelve Cycles before, at the end of the first Jubilee Period, the narrator has threatened the reader with this weird title ("obbligato leaf"), and now he laughs at him mockingly for not having noticed that he was being exposed to this frightening experience.

A discussion of the style of *Titan* cannot end without a passing note on Jean Paul's naming of the main divisions of the novel, normally called chapters. We have mentioned the "Dog-Post-Days" in *Hesperus*. *The Invisible Lodge*, on the other hand, is simply divided into "Sectors," a term taken from geometry, while *Quintus Fixlein* consists of fourteen "Filing-Cabinets" and one "Last Chapter," assuring the reader that the history is not invented but true. *The Parson in Jubilee* has "Official Reports" alternating with "Pastoral- and Circle-Letters"—very appropriately so since the protagonist of the story is a minister. Jean Paul's autobiography consists of "Lectures" (see p. 18); *The Life of Fibel* has the most humorous chapter titles referring to the misuse of the original manuscript (see p. 37); and *The Twins* takes its chapter titles from the pieces of a mineral collection.

In *Titan,* Jean Paul uses the "Jubilee Period" and subdivides it
into "Cycles." The Old Testament "Jubilee Years" came every
twenty-five years and were heralded by trumpets. According to
the narrator, it was Franke, Jr., the Rector, who defined the
Jubilee Period of 152 cycles, "each of which contains itself its
good forty-nine tropical Lunar-Solar years. . . ." "I make a sufficiently happy application of his title," the author continues,
"to my historical chapters, which conduct the businessman and
the businesswoman round and round in an easy cycle full of free
Sabbath-, Indulgence-, Trumpet-, and Jubilee-hours, in which
both have neither to sow nor to pay, but only to ripen and to
rest" (I, 57).

But in the midst of this learned and humorous attack on his
lazy readers—nowadays we would call them a typical television
audience asking for predigested food—the narrator waxes serious
by raising the much discussed problem of time. For him ideas
determine the time value of the individual chapters and are the
"long and cubic measure of time." Therefore, each chapter contains as many ideas as are needed to keep the reader busy, as
long as Jean Paul thinks he should be: "The seven thousand four
hundred forty-nine tropical Lunar-Solar years which one of
Franke's Jubilee Periods includes are also found with me, but
only dramatically, because in every chapter just that number of
ideas will be presented by me to the reader, till the short time
has become as long to him as the chapter required" (I, 57).

The figure of the narrator offers the best opportunity to explain Jean Paul's concept of humor, which he defines as the
finite projected on the infinite.[33] What does he mean with this
synthesis of polar elements? Käte Hamburger replaces the infinite by the world of ideas or the "Great and Essential"; and the
finite by the world of objects, or the "Small and Unessential."
The function of wit is, then, to degrade the Great, and that of
humor to elevate the Small, so that they touch each other and
are both annihilated, because all is equal, or nothing, before the
infinite. Thus Swift's "Vive la bagatelle!" stresses one side of
humor—the concentration on small things surrounding us—
which counterbalances the dreams of our magic imagination.[34]

Humor progresses from discontent with this world of particulars via discontent with the incongruity between the ego
and the external objects to the incongruity between the ego and

the mind.[35] Through laughter, the mind is liberated and experiences a subjective deliverance from everything ugly and limiting. "To man . . . looking down from the metaphysical world to the physical one the latter appears small and vain; when he measures and pieces together the infinite with the help of the finite, which is done by humor, then that kind of laughter will come into being that contains pain and greatness." [36]

When we apply Jean Paul's definition of humor to his style we see why the structure of his novels is "more allegorical than realistic," it being so designed as to bring about "the humorous confrontation of areas of life . . . with the help of which the value, or lack of value, of man can be humorously revealed." [37] From the viewpoint of humor, it becomes evident that the plot and the characters are important only insofar as they can, in Böckmann's words, "measure out the potential relation between the finite and the infinite. . . . Humor places before man the problem of the infinite by calling forth the contrast between the finite and the infinite" (p. 53). Böckmann coined the very helpful phrase "refractive relation" ("Brechungsbeziehung") between the objective content and its subjective reader—a relation which is personified in the humorous attitude of the narrator. Humor, then, is a refractive relation between content and reader, a subjective rendering of experience or vision that receives its special illumination from the narrator's point of view. No statement has value in itself; only Jean Paul's *way* of stating creates the manifold relations which contribute to the humorous tone. As Böckmann puts it, "In all his works we find this style of continuous refraction. . . . The relations of life and death, man and nature . . . past and present are always reflected. . . . [They] point back to the narrator and make visible his attitude toward such a life. . . . He is present in every single word" (pp. 47–48).

CHAPTER 5

Siebenkäs

I Development of Plot, Characters, and Themes

JEAN PAUL'S *Siebenkäs* is the first German realistic middle-class novel after Grimmelshausen's *Simplizissimus* (1669); it is also the first important novel to present the problems of married life, for Goethe's *Elective Affinities* was not published until 1809, eleven years after the first edition of *Siebenkäs*.[1] The first of the three volumes was written in 1795 in a great hurry, under the pressure of inspiration. "I have hardly time to sneeze," Jean Paul wrote jokingly to his friend Christian Otto.[2] In nine months he had finished the novel, which consisted of three volumes in the first edition, and of four volumes in the second and enlarged edition of 1817–18.

According to Jean Paul, the nucleus of the novel is *My Own Funeral*, a first sketch of which was written in 1789. The problem of death, presented by Jean Paul in various ways—as the apparent death of Ottomar in *The Invisible Lodge*, as the predetermined death of Emanuel in *Hesperus*, and as Fixlein's fear of dying on a certain day in *Quintus Fixlein*—has also influenced the plot and tenor of this novel which, according to the original plan, was almost farcical.[3]

In the early version, the narrator, a lawyer, is married to Fike, a simple housewife. On a business trip, he meets a girl who is nobly born, intelligent, proud, and very poor, and whom he tries to help, at least financially, by taking out a so-called widow's insurance in her name. This could be done, at that time, by any relative or friend of a young woman, and not only by her husband. In any case, she became the beneficiary after the man's death. Long before he wrote this story Jean Paul had been intrigued by this fact and had made a note of it in his excerpts. When Fike hears about this insurance in behalf of another woman, she gets so jealous and her married life becomes so unhappy that she agrees to her husband's plan to fake his death, which gives her the freedom to elope with a well-situated minister and school supervisor whom she prefers greatly to her complicated husband.[4]

The final version of the plot is so different from this early one that it is hardly recognizable, although the faked death and the widow's insurance still figure in it. But the main theme of the final version is the gradual destruction of the mutual love of the married couple, caused by the characters of the lovers and not by external events. The aristocratic girl—Natalie in the final version—meets Siebenkäs only after his love for his wife Lenette has been thoroughly destroyed by their incompatibility. Lenette Wendeline, the most realistic female character ever created by Jean Paul, is an excellent housewife, very attractive, religious, and faithful, but narrow-minded and without any spiritual interest or understanding for things outside the pattern of petty-bourgeois life. She is incapable of any depth of feeling and any enthusiasm that would carry her beyond her own little world. Like Tristram Shandy's mother, who asks her husband whether he forgot to wind the clock at a moment when she should be in seventh heaven lying in her husband's arms, Lenette goes right on sewing while her husband kisses her. She is ashamed of her poverty and is deeply hurt that she cannot serve a goose on St. Martin's Day, which is the right of any good Lutheran. Her only reading material is the cookbook, and she does not even try to read her husband's works, although she admires him for being a "bookmaker." She needs social and financial security before she is capable of loving a man and longs for a husband who behaves conventionally, goes to church, and makes enough money to provide for her needs and desires. She finds all this in Stiefel, the local minister and school supervisor.

Her husband and his friend Leibgeber, on the other hand, despise middle-class feelings and ideas and do not care what people think of them. They disdain all egoistical motivations and calculated actions and want to be free to follow their imagination and their impulses. They love all really good people and endure stoically their poverty and the scorn of their bourgeois neighbors. Leibgeber precedes Siebenkäs in this attitude, which he has already achieved at the beginning of the novel, whereas Siebenkäs frees himself only step by step. This struggle of Siebenkäs's may be considered the second theme of the novel, which lends dramatic tension to the friendship of the two men and justifies Siebenkäs's death as the final liberation of the man who plays freely with all the bonds of life, including death.

In the *Introduction to Esthetics*, Jean Paul discusses the creation of the characters in his novels. According to him, writing is like giving birth: "Each poet gives birth to his special individual angel and to his special devil, so to speak, the ideal ego of the poet's ego. The poet can be recognized in his protagonists." [5] This theory fits perfectly the creation of Leibgeber and Siebenkäs, two friends who are so much alike that they are virtually one. They have symbolic reality, which means for Jean Paul that they are no longer individuals but representatives of specific aspects of mankind. Leibgeber and Siebenkäs have "one basic color, one *primum mobile*, one *tonica dominante*," [6] which is absolute freedom of all petty-bourgeois interests, and love for all suffering human beings—the latter being Jean Paul's basic postulate for religion. Jean Paul reasons that man must be immortal because his feeling for other human beings, be it love between man and woman, between friends, or among all men, is so strong and so patently the only value in life that it simply cannot be destroyed by death.

If Leibgeber and Siebenkäs represent Jean Paul's "special individual angel," his extreme longing for freedom that may end even in self-destruction (Schoppe in *Titan* is another manifestation of this "angel"), then Lenette Wendeline represents his "special devil," the petty-bourgeois type in essence.

The book represents a psychological study of the diminution and destruction of married love. There are fights and reconciliations; Siebenkäs tries to be fair to Lenette and save her unnecessary suffering; but finally jealousy of Stiefel, the lucky rival, and the realization that everything Lenette does hurts his feelings (whether she cleans the room or does not clean it, whether she keeps quiet or is noisy, whether she makes him wait for his coffee or serves the soup in the wrong moment) force him to admit that staying with her will ruin him completely. For Lenette, the progress is from a father-daughter relationship of esteem and submissiveness to indifference and, finally, misery. She truly suffers from their poverty, as well as from her total incomprehension of her husband's character. She is afraid that he is an atheist because he does not go to church and does not believe in processions, whether led by Lutheran ministers or Catholic priests. Lenette, of course, only doubts the validity of the latter. Finally she suffers as well from jealousy when she learns about Natalie, her husband's beautiful and intelligent protégée. But long before this last stage in her married life, she has fallen in love with Stiefel without knowing it.

The solution to the problems of the married couple devolves from the second theme, the friendship between Leibgeber and Siebenkäs. Leibgeber concocts gleefully a scheme whereby Siebenkäs is to pretend to die. But Jean Paul did not want to shock his reader with this cynical denouement. Leibgeber therefore curses himself later for having begun the farce when he sees Lenette's real despair at her husband's death. From the beginning Siebenkäs himself earnestly and sincerely wishes to die. His subsequent life in another town, Vaduz, is miserable enough, because he has lost Lenette to Stiefel, and because he has sworn never to see either Natalie or Leibgeber again. His only satisfaction is the recognition of his work, which is, of course, attributed to Leibgeber, whose identity he assumes in Vaduz. The late and accidental reunion of Siebenkäs and Natalie at Lenette's grave, after Lenette has died in childbirth, is like a scene set in another world. Natalie almost dies when she recognizes Siebenkäs, whom she has mourned for a year; and he clutches the two roses which Natalie had given him a year ago so tightly that blood from the wounds caused by the thorns covers his hand. This is certainly not a happy ending; however, Natalie's words, "Eternity is in this world," seem to point to the triumph of love over death, which gives, metaphysically speaking, a happy ending to the novel as a whole.

The life of Siebenkäs is the genuine "Thorn Piece" of the novel, whose full title is *Flower, Fruit and Thorn Pieces: or the Married Life, Death, and Wedding of the Advocate of the Poor, Firmian Stanislaus Siebenkäs in the Imperial Market-Town of Kuhschnappel.* The first "Flower-Piece" is the famous "Speech of the Dead Christ from Heaven That There Is No God" which, in the first edition, stood at the beginning of the novel but in the second edition was moved to the center of the work. This "Speech" allows an interpretation of the novel from a religious point of view. Writing it, Jean Paul worked himself into a state of terror. The setting—a dark church at midnight; Christ preaching to the dead; the laments of the children bereft of the image of a loving father—all this was so terrifying for Jean Paul that we believe in his relief when the nightmare was finally over and he could trust God again and be thankful for his existence. The nightmare is vividly convincing, and the two points of view, religious and atheistic, give the novel depth.

Siebenkäs believes in immortality and exhorts his friend Leibgeber to believe in it as well, because how else, he argues, can there be eternal love? But Leibgeber, who is as convincing a character as Siebenkäs, cannot do so. At Siebenkäs's open grave he urges the "hidden Infinite One" to transform the grave into a prompter's box, so that he may learn what to think of the whole play. This is certainly more a challenge than a prayer.

In his study on Jean Paul and Dostoevski Walter Rehm carries out a profound analysis of Jean Paul's religious approach.[7] He compares Leibgeber's attitude to the *experimentum suae medietatis* of Saint Augustine, an attempt to make the Ego the center of the world, instead of hating it which, according to Pascal, should be our only virtue. In Rehm's view, Jean Paul is not one of the famous anti-saints of earlier times, like Theophilus, Simon Magus, Cenodoxus, and Dr. Faustus, who deny the existence of God; nor is he one of the "monks of atheism" as Heine calls his contemporaries, Büchner, Kierkegaard, J. P. Jacobsen, or the French authors Musset, Flaubert, Baudelaire, who live in despair because, as Büchner says, "Le Néant is the chaos to be born . . . le Néant has committed suicide." [8]

Jean Paul knew very well the despair of the true atheist; and he has Schoppe in *Titan* predict his "ascension to the future nothingness . . . to death after his death." [9] He himself, however, must have found his way back to a religious attitude because he claims that the epic poet can only create a world of his own if he feels the underlying harmony and beauty of the created world. Gottfried Keller is describing a parallel revelation in Chapter Twenty of *The Green Henry*, when the young painter-protagonist discovers a young beech to be so clear and beautiful, so charged with life and God, that he must recreate it on paper.[10]

II *Analysis of Style*

The reader who is willing to concentrate on a novel like *Siebenkäs* must have time and patience to read and reread the text because Jean Paul does no spoon-feeding and requires the reader himself to perform a creative act, i.e., re-create with his own imagination the world of the poet. In a sense, as Wolfgang Kayser points out, the author even creates his reader who must be willing to follow patiently through Jean Paul's elaborate schemata of images, allusions, comparisons, and puns in order to gain the author's insight and share his emotions.[11] Jean Paul helps us to do this by means of certain stylistic techniques. Thus he avoids abstract nouns, and eschews intransitive verbs in favor of transitive ones. He does not use Klopstock's famous comparatives because they do not engage the senses. He cultivates the strong impulse produced by the use, in German, of prepositions governing the accusative case instead of the dative. He uses compounds rather than descriptive adjectives, the latter being effective only when they result from inspiration as in the case of Goethe, examples from whose works Jean Paul quotes in the *Introduction to Esthetics* (§ 82). It might be useful to give a few illustrations of Jean Paul's style by analyzing a page from *Siebenkäs* and pointing out some typical stylistic features.[12]

Returning from Bayreuth where, influenced by Leibgeber, he has decided on his faked death and where he has met and lost Natalie forever, Siebenkäs approaches his home, full of love for Lenette, to whom he still feels a strong attachment, in spite of his decision to leave her.

He hastened on more speedily, passed close by the window-shutters of his fellow commander Merbitzer, and bent back his head to look at the windows above.

[Er drängte sich mit zurückgekrümmtem, nach den obern Fenstern blickendem Kopf an den Fensterladen seines Neben-Kommandeurs Merbitzer vorbei.]

He forced his way not *through* which would be the normal phrase, but *past* the shutters. Most probably they are closed; for otherwise Jean Paul would have Siebenkäs hurry past the *windows.* The compound descriptive adjectives "curved backwards" and "looking towards," both participles, almost force us to bend our heads in the same uncomfortable way he does. Merbitzer owns the house. He is Siebenkäs's "co-commander" because the two shared the honor of being crowned champions at the bird shooting match in the second volume. With this one humorous metaphor Jean Paul conjures up the past; the couple's miserable life before the shooting match, the excitement of the match itself and, finally, the gay abandon of the festival that followed—summing up the climax of the second volume in a single word. Here, as in all the following excerpts from the scene, each sentence—in fact each metaphor—is heavily charged with the characters' common past, with intensity but not with bitterness, so that the reader identifies fully with the protagonist, experiencing exactly the same feelings—in fact climbing the same stairs.

The latter was splitting wood on Sabbath, and Firmian made him a sign not to betray him by any sentinel-cry; the old co-tsar nodded in answer, with outstretched fingers, that Lenette was upstairs in her chamber alone.

[Dieser spaltete im Hause Sabbatholz, und Firmian winkte, ihn durch kein Schildwachengeschrei zu verraten; der alte Nebenzar winkte sogleich mit ausgestreckten Fingern zurück, Lenette sei nämlich allein oben in der Stube.]

"Sabbatical wood," wood cut on a Sabbath (a compound invented by Jean Paul) is witty because a person to whose vocabulary the word "Sabbath" belongs would not, for religious reasons, cut wood on that day. The Lutheran Merbitzer thus forms a humorous contrast to the imaginary orthodox Jew, and by means of this implication Jean Paul makes us smile. "The sentinel-cry," another compound metaphor, again has a humorous effect because of the incongruity between the image and the harmless Siebenkäs, who is not a dangerous enemy but a loving husband who wants to surprise his wife. "Co-tsar," a new compound, is self-contradictory in itself since a tsar is an absolute monarch. It is used parallel to "co-commander," thus assigning a rise in rank to the old champion shot. Merbitzer does not simply wave at Siebenkäs, but in a more expressive and emphatic way he "waves back" with "outstretched fingers," forcing our imagination to follow the direction of his fingers, so that we understand, like Siebenkäs, that Lenette is home.

The old well known ripieno voices of the house, the quarrelsome screeching of the bookbinder's wife, the subdued singing of the passionate prayer-mouther and curser Fecht, met him, like sweet fodder, as he sneaked up the stairs.

[Die alten gewohnten Ripienstimmen des Hauses, das zankende Gellen der Buchbinderin, der Sing-Dämpfer des eifrigen Beters und Fluchers Fecht, fiel ihm unter dem Hinaufschleichen der Treppe wie süsses Futter entgegen.]

"The old well known ripieno voices of the house," a metaphor from Baroque music (*ripieno* meaning the orchestral accompaniment as distinct from the solo) will send most readers to the dictionary; but what is essential is that there is not a single melody but a full, rich background sound. *Ripieno* is further described appositively as yelling reinforced by the participle "quarreling," and by "mute," said not of a violin but of a "singing" voice, which is again enriched by the antithesis of "prayer-mouther and curser." All these sounds are not heard by Siebenkäs, but they "fall upon" him like "sweet fodder," thus implying an animal's happily unconscious gulping of food, i.e., while climbing silently upstairs Siebenkäs is filled with happy associations by all these familiar noises. But how boring and unimpressive is this long colorless explanation compared with Jean Paul's rich sentence, where the reader should slowly savor each word as a winetaster chews a good wine.

The waning moon of his movable pewter property shone on him from the kitchen gloriously bright and silvery. Everything had arisen fresh scoured out of the bath of regeneration. A copper fish-kettle, which, as long as it remained unmended, could not poison any vinegar, glowed upon him through the smoke of the kitchen-fire, like the sun through a halo.

[Der abnehmende Mond seiner fahrenden Zinnhabe glänzte aus der Küche ihm herrlich und silbern entgegen, alles war gescheuert aus dem Bade der Wiedergeburt gestiegen, eine kupferne Fischpfanne— die so lange keinen Essig vergiftet, als man sie nicht flicken liess— glühte ihn aus dem Küchenrauch des Einheizens, wie die Sonne aus dem Heerrauch, an.]

"The waning moon of his movable tin-goods" is again humorous, meaning that Siebenkäs is losing his property as the moon loses her fullness. The tin-goods are *movable* because Siebenkäs takes them to the pawnshop when he needs money, and brings them home as soon as he can afford to do so. The one word "movable" summarizes the story of the financial difficulties of the couple, of Lenette's anguish about her poverty and her husband's lack of interest in money. The tinplates shine "towards" him marvelously and silvery—the preposition "towards" bringing movement into the static world of the kitchen. The "bath of regeneration" hints in a humorous way at Lenette's exaggerated cleanliness, a fact which made Siebenkäs happy as long as he was in love, and drove him out of his mind after the honeymoon was over.

"A copper fish-kettle, which, as long as it remained unmended, could not poison any vinegar, glowed upon him . . . like the sun [verbally] out of a smoke caused by an army." The witty comparison of the smoke of a kitchen fire and that of army fires is easily grasped. Even the pan that cannot poison as long as it is not mended is not a puzzle for the dedicated reader of Jean Paul. With the happy smile of the mathematician who deciphers a secret formula he understands that the pan cannot be used, apparently because it has a hole. Therefore vinegar cannot be poured into it, so that the chemical process of copper and acid producing poison will not take place. Again we are told indirectly and humorously that Siebenkäs and Lenette are so poor that they cannot pay for the repair of the pan.

He opened the door of the sitting-room gently, saw that no one was in, and heard Lenette making the bed in the chamber.

[Er zog leise die Stubentüre auf, er sah niemand darin und hörte Lenetten in der Kammer betten.]

Siebenkäs does not simply open the door but "pulls it open" gently, this being a slow movement to prevent Lenette from hearing him. He does not see her in the living room but hears her in the small bedroom, a fact which adds tension to the introduction of the homecoming scene. He hears her making the bed. Here Jean Paul uses a verb derived from the noun "bed," so that Siebenkäs hears Lenette "bedding," a verb that is as unusual in German as it is in English. At the moment of his return, Lenette is preparing the place where he feels most protected and where all his writing takes place. The intimacy of the bedroom is a better setting for a homecoming scene than either the kitchen or the living room.

With a hammer-knocking in his bosom, he made a long and gentle stride into the clean apartment, which had already put on its Sunday shirt of white sand, and on which the bed-making river-goddess and water-nymph had expended all her water-skill to make it a finished work of art.

[Er tat, mit einem Hammerwerk in der Brust, einen weiten leisen Schritt in die geputzte Stube, die schon ein Sonntaghemde aus weissem Sand angelegt und woran die bettende Flussgöttin und Wassernymphe alle Wasserkünste versucht hatte zu einem ausgefeilten Kunstwerk.]

The "ironworks" (in German "hammer" works) in his breast describing his hammering heart is a popular metaphor in German, but the hero's "long careful step" into the living room adds motion; and the metaphors of the goddess of bedding and rivers, the water nymph and her fountains that have produced the Sunday shirt of white sand—all of them make fun in a friendly way of Lenette, the cleanest housewife ever, who uses too much water for her housework. The closer we approach the moment of reunion, the more we see Lenette with the eyes of Siebenkäs who is still aware of her shortcomings but does not feel any bitterness, only a sympathetic understanding of her character, which is so different from his own.

How peacefully and harmoniously everything reposed, the one thing near the other, after the business and bustle of the week! The rain-star had risen over everything, his inkstand alone was dried up.

[Ach, alles ruhte so einträchtig vom Gewühle der Woche aus. Über alles war das Regengestirn aufgegangen, nur sein Tintenfass war eingetrocknet.]

The objects in the room are personified and have a special mood of peace and harmony like human beings. The "rain-star," a word coined by Jean Paul to parallel "rainbow," fits into the series of water metaphors used earlier. The dryness of Siebenkäs's inkwell is noted, but he does not suffer from this negligence on Lenette's part, in whose life ink is of no importance whatever. —At the climax of this carefully prepared scene, when Siebenkäs holds Lenette in his arms, she pushes him back, embarrassed, because Stiefel, Siebenkäs's rival, enters. This last chance for a reconciliation is thus spoiled by her self-conscious reaction and Stiefel's interference.

It goes without saying that each character in a Jean Paul novel speaks a language of his own. Even without knowing the name of the person speaking we would, for instance, recognize Lenette with her simplicity, charm, naïveté and simple, vulgar sentimentality. At the moment of her death she asks: "I shall go to where Firmian is, shall I not?" [13] Natalie's words show understanding, depth, and a touch of humor when she recognizes Siebenkäs in the churchyard after she has heard his confession: "You sacrificed yourself for other people's happiness. Now you will make up for all your betrayals." [14] Stiefel, the superintendent of schools, speaks and writes a dry, colorless office German, whereas Leibgeber seems to use the purest Jean Paul vocabulary and style which is also used by Siebenkäs, but more poetically and with a better balance.

The reader who enjoys the style of Rabelais, and Shakespeare should have no difficulties reading Jean Paul. All three authors love to play with language, endowing it liberally with witty puns, far-fetched comparisons, and complex metaphors, giving it freshness and novelty, so that each word, or at least its sense, appears to be altogether original.

In the *Introduction to Esthetics*, Jean Paul distinguishes between the romantic-epic and the romantic-dramatic novel, the former, like Goethe's *Wilhelm Meister*, having the world as protagonist, whereas the latter, like the novels of Richardson, Fielding, Wieland, and Jean Paul, concentrates on characters and not on the "playing field or scope of history" ("Spielraum der Geschichte").[15] This dramatic form forces the author to create scenes of tension and dramatic climax, and to describe characters and motivations clearly and sharply. The relation between action and character is best explained by Jean Paul's own metaphor, that they are like body and soul, the soul forming the body but unable to exist without it.

In *Siebenkäs* the action is secondary, the main stress being on the characters, who are portrayed as *feeling* and *thinking*, so that their activities are only side effects. Because Leibgeber and Siebenkäs are such close friends that they want to share everything, even their names, they exchange them. This gives the first impulse to the plot: having taken another name, Siebenkäs loses his heritage. Because Lenette cannot exist without financial security her love comes to an end when she learns about the loss of the family's money through Siebenkäs's fault. Because Leibgeber is absolutely free of all social and religious restrictions, he suggests that his friend should pretend to die. Because Siebenkäs sees in love the perfect mystical union of two human beings, his love for Lenette ends when he realizes that there is

no equivalent response on her part. According to modern classi-
fication, Jean Paul's novels belong to the group of "novels of
characters" [16] in which the characters are delineated at the beginning of the story and the later action offers an opportunity
for the reader to get acquainted with their specific traits. Stanzel
defines Jean Paul's novels as "auctorial", i.e., the narrator is always present, interrupting the story constantly, commenting and
evaluating the thoughts and actions so that the reader sees the
characters through the author's eyes, the author being the arbiter
between the fictitious world of the novel and the real world of
the reader. By his interference, he splits the novel in two parts,
the novel *per se* and an essay-like discussion of the novel.[17]

The nineteenth century objected to this view as the propo-
nents of realism preferred the "personal" novel, in which the
author was silent, giving, so to speak, an objective report and
leaving the interpretation entirely to the reader.[18] The twentieth-
century reader, however, who is well trained by modern authors
to regard the effect of alienation ("Verfremdung") as a positive
value, understands more easily that the auctorial novel has its
raison d'être as well as the personal novel or even the first-person
novel. In the latter, the narrator, who is not necessarily identical
with the author, is part of the fictitious world and reports his
own deeds and feelings in an attempt to understand himself and
his relations with others and with the world: This attempt at
self-understanding gives the novel a certain pathos.[19] *Siebenkäs*,
although basically an auctorial novel, is sometimes close to the
first-person novel, i.e., whenever the narrator relates himself to
the characters of the story. In both cases, whether contemplating
the fictitious world from a distance or reliving it in his memory,
the author creates a harmonious, and as it were, classical world,
after having led us through disorder and chaos. Time is Jean
Paul's principal device in bringing order into the world of the
novel. We are constantly informed about the month and the day
of the week as if the author had worked with a calendar in his
hand.

The second edition of *Siebenkäs* was published twenty years
after the first, in 1817 and 1818. Originally the novel, divided
into three parts, began with the two "Flower-Pieces": "Speech
of the Dead Christ from Heaven That There Is No God" and
"The Dream in the Dream." The first "Fruit-Painting" followed

the fourth chapter whereas it now concludes the third volume; the two "Flower-Pieces" now stand at the end of the second volume. This rearrangement was necessary because, with the division into four parts and the general enlargement of the novel, the first volume would have been too long. The original break, Siebenkäs leaving Kuhschnappel in order to meet Leibgeber in Bayreuth, came at the beginning of the third volume; this was certainly more organic than the present version where the break occurs in the middle of the third volume. However, in spite of the new division, each volume builds up its own tension. The first one takes us from the wedding day through the honeymoon to the equinox and the "first thunderstorm" at the beginning of the fourth chapter, when Lenette learns of the loss of Siebenkäs's fortune, and from there to the masterful description of Siebenkäs drawing Lenette's silhouette as a gift for Stiefel, when Siebenkäs realizes that Lenette has perhaps never loved him but appears unconsciously in love with Stiefel.

The second volume describes the constant battle of the married couple broken by short moments of peace. At the end of this volume, we find Lenette, Siebenkäs, and Stiefel at the cemetery; Lenette cries and leans her head on Stiefel's shoulder, incapable of giving her hand to Siebenkäs as a sign of reconciliation, because she shudders with loathing at the thought that he held a skull with these same hands a few moments ago. The third volume, relating Siebenkäs's love for Natalie, has its climax at the moment of her farewell kiss. And the fourth volume, describing Siebenkäs's simulated death, ends with another scene at the cemetery where Siebenkäs and Natalie are reunited.

The very end of the novel leaves the reader, for the first time, to his emotions and gives him no help in struggling back to the real world. There are no helpful digressions to ease him back to earth, no learned or poetic essays on religion or philanthropy, no direct or indirect attacks on, or exhortations to, the reader or non-reader. Jean Paul abruptly stops the incessant see-saw between tragic and farcical aspects, which has so strained the reader's equilibrium, and changes his tone to that of a "personal" novel, compelling us to serious reflection and perhaps directing our understanding to deeper layers of the cosmos which we might otherwise overlook.

CHAPTER 6

Walt and Vult; *or* The Twins

I *Basic Structure*

WHEREAS the modern reader experiences almost insurmountable difficulties in finishing the four volumes of *Titan*, he is well capable of enjoying Jean Paul's other masterpiece, the unfinished novel with the untranslatable title, *Die Flegeljahre*. For the early nineteenth century this meant the years when the adolescent is uncertain of himself, easily embarrassed, bashful, and in his confusion sometimes rude, aggressive, and clumsy; years which are characterized by a heightened intensity of feeling both pleasure and pain, an intensity which the more sophisticated adult no longer experiences. Biologically, Gottwalt Harnisch, the novel's protagonist, has passed through adolescence and should be finished with his *Flegeljahre*, for at the beginning of the novel, he is twenty-four years old and just about to take his last examination in law. He has finished his courses at Leipzig University, where every term he studied diligently until sheer hunger drove him home. He now wants to settle down in Hasslau, a small town near his native village of Elterlein, where his old teacher Schomaker, a man of great learning, still represents one of his happiest associations.

But in spite of the fact that he is at the beginning of his career, Walt (a short form for Gottwalt) is still in the midst of his *Flegeljahre*. He is a young poet living in a world of his own and incapable of coping with everyday problems; an innocent who turns the small hand of the clock in order to move the large hand. He loves mankind and is born for the church, but is too weak to resist the insistent wishes of his parents, who want him to go into law. Walt is so devoted to his parents that he will do anything they wish except give up writing poetry. When his writing is maligned he turns into a god of wrath.

The same immaturity shows in Walt's emotional reactions: for he forgets his timidity, his professional duties, and even his love for his twin brother Vult in order to pursue a passionate and ill-fated friendship with an aristocrat, Klothar, who spurns him. An essentially good person, who has to overcome some weaknesses before he can be considered a man of character, Walt is, in a way, Jean Paul himself, but only *that* part of his personality which was adored by his female readers and by very young men, all of whom were caught up in the spirit of "Empfindsamkeit" (sensibility). All had identified themselves with the ideas presented in *The Invisible Lodge* and in *Hesperus,* and did not appreciate Jean Paul's condemnation of all eccentricity, even that of feeling, in *Titan.*

Jean Paul's other side, the highly intelligent, witty, sardonic, misanthropic, Leibgeber-Schoppe-Giannozzo type, appears here as Walt's twin brother Vult (Quod Deus Vult or Whatever God Wants were the words his father uttered after Walt's birth when it became apparent that a second child was to be expected). Vult is Walt's opposite in appearance and in character. Whereas Walt is fair-haired, blue-eyed, pale, and delicate, Vult is dark, vigorous, obstinate, and resilient, a great fighter, born for the law. He hates all discipline, at fourteen runs away with a poor flute player and devotes all of his young life to a flute worth ten cents.

The purpose of the novel is to achieve a synthesis of these two characters, the development of Walt towards maturity, with a realistic view of this world, even to the point of being capable of hating somebody, and of Vult's giving in to his love for those to whom he belongs, freeing himself of the dangerous isolation that leads characters like Schoppe, Giannozzo, and himself to self-destruction.[1]

In order to give an internal structure to this development of two antipodes, and in order to maintain the proper tension, Jean Paul begins the first chapter with the reading of a Mr. Van der Kabel's last will, which makes Walt the heir of properties and a great fortune, but he has to fulfill sixteen more or less absurd stipulations before he receives the inheritance. Seven disinherited heirs, his guardians, and his best enemies, wishing him bad luck and intriguing against him, do all they can to ruin him. With the delineation of these heirs, who act as a group inimical to Walt, with the story of Count Klothar and Wina, both of them loved by Walt, with Vult's jealousy, despair, and final departure when he finds out that Walt and Wina do not return his feelings —with all these strands Jean Paul creates a basic structure that keeps the reader's interest alive. Within this framework, he allows himself to stress characters, descriptions, and reflections rather than the development of the plot. Occasionally he altogether forgets about the framework of his novel and the reader does the same until Jean Paul continues the story, a fact which, in itself, is of minor importance to us and to him.

For ten years, from 1795 to 1805, Jean Paul enjoyed writing this novel whenever he had time to recover from his "Italian" novel, *Titan*. For some time he actually planned to combine the two novels, having one chapter of *Titan* followed by one of *Flegeljahre*. Eduard Berend gives a detailed description of six working periods, showing the different developmental stages of this novel, which allows us to have a look into Jean Paul's workshop, where he is busy with characters and motivations, but hardly ever with the plot.[2]

In the first draft, written between 1795 and 1799, the main character is conceived as another Wutz, who is grateful for small things, happy in his modest home, a dreamer and a poet, shy, naïve, loving all mankind, but especially attracted to aristocrats. Playing in a lottery this idyllic character is faced with the sudden acquisition of a great fortune. He has to change his social status, but his new life of leisure does not make him happy. He buys a castle, goes bankrupt; but before he loses his fortune he makes himself the minister of the community belonging to the castle he is about to sell, for to choose the minister of a village was formerly the right of the German landowner. This first version of the novel reminds us somewhat of the Grimm fairy tale of "Hans im Glück," a happy-go-lucky boy who gladly exchanges his burdensome gold bar for a goose. Jean Paul did not make a final decision about the structure of this first version of the novel, i.e., whether one experience should follow another in the picaresque style, or whether there should be an integration of the action with a resulting tension as in *Siebenkäs*. Judged by standards valid for the world of *Titan*, the hero of this first version was a "negative" Titan, a learned, absent-minded innocent too naïve to grasp reality.

During the second working period, from April through May, 1801(after the completion of the second volume of *Titan*), Jean

Paul gave his hero a name, Blitz (lightning). But the real center of this character was not yet defined. Jean Paul made him a lawyer, thus forcing him to find his way into real life through his career.

Jean Paul's own wedding interrupted his work on the book, but in the following year he returned to "The Story of My Twin Brother," introducing himself as the second character of the novel, and planning a sublimated version of the burlesque story of the twin brothers included in the *Comic Appendix to Titan*. Peter and Seraph are physically inseparable, representing the body and soul of one being. They would destroy each other if their father had not forced them, by his last will, to give full power of decision to each of them for one day only. In this third version of the novel, Jean Paul planned to describe autobiographically his insatiable love for reading, his own skepticism and pessimism, and his search for a publisher.

The two brothers Richter of the novel write "The Book of the Judges"—a pun with Jean Paul's last name (Richter meaning judge)—which they try desperately to publish. The first chapter describes the flute player's journey home, the brother's examination, and the first meeting and recognition of the twin brothers in a churchyard; i.e., Chapters Five through Thirteen of the actual novel.

But not before the fourth working period, December, 1802, through May, 1803, did Jean Paul find the focus for Walt's character, the secret spiritual center of his life, namely his poetic imagination, contrasted with Vult's harsh rationalism; and his humanitarianism, contrasted with Vult's egotism. Thus the first three volumes of the novel were sketched, and between June and October, in 1803, they were completed and titled *Die Flegeljahre*. They were published in May, 1804, showing Jean Paul's last name Richter on the title page for the first and the last time in his life.

The fourth volume, written in 1805, after the completion of the *Introduction to Esthetics*, centers around Vult's love for Wina, who feels more attracted to young Parzival, that is, Walt, on account of his innocence, purity, and naïveté. Vult leaves forever. However, the novel was never finished, although Jean Paul had enough material for many more volumes. He could not solve the basic problem, since the union of the two antipodes

Walt and Vult was out of his reach. But a solution was hardly Jean Paul's innermost motivation for writing this novel; for the different stages show the interest he took in the characters, their moods, and their motivations. He was satisfied when he forced his readers to think about problems and perhaps understand life better than they had before reading his novels.

The actual writing of *Flegeljahre* did not take Jean Paul more than ten months after he had found a perfect plot, and after he had shaped the characters and their motivations for almost ten years. Knowing so well what, on the one side, his readers expected from him and what, on the other side, he had to say in his own way, he did not actually change his style. However, he avoided shocking his readers by giving up his famous digressions, unnecessary footnotes, endless comparisons, and his exhibition of odd erudition—all of which is still to be found in *The Twins*, but incorporated into the texture of the novel, so that the reader can swallow it more easily.

II *Footnotes*

This inclination toward classicism can be recognized, e.g., by considering the use of footnotes in *The Twins*, a subject which Walter Rehm has dealt with in one of the best essays on Jean Paul in recent years.[3] For Jean Paul it was a recreation to write introductions, epilogues, interludes, and footnotes after having told the actual story—a labor which he compared to "a ship of slaves."[4] Novalis's remark that a note referring to a text is more stimulating than the text itself could just as well have been made by him. Novalis's words sound jocular, but since Cervantes's ironical criticism of footnotes we have known that they form an important structural element of the epic work by adding a new dimension and perspective to the different strata of a novel. The triangular relationship between the storyteller, the work, and the reader is easily enhanced by the use of footnotes which invite the reader to take an active part in "playing" with the ingredients of the work, swinging from the upper part of the page to the lines at the bottom and back again, and only by so imitating the movements of the author can we understand his irony.[5]

Whereas in the baroque novel footnotes were taken seriously, because the reader wanted to gain encyclopedic knowledge through his study of great authors,[6] Jean Paul invites the reader to play for the sake of playing, the contents of the notes being negligible for the understanding of the text. He goes so far as to insert footnotes without any relevance to the text, apologizing for the error of the printer who got them mixed up before he began working on his idyll *Trip of the Military Chaplain Schmelzle to Flätz* (1809). Actually, Jean Paul's famous excerpts from the books he read were published in his footnotes. For him any fact was important; and he could have said like Leibniz: "Je ne méprise presque rien." [7] However, the general reader is obviously more interested in the characters than in minor or merely curious facts. Knowing this, the mature Jean Paul refrained from the exaggerated use of footnotes. In *Siebenkäs*, there is one footnote on every third page, in *Flegeljahre* on every ninth page only.

Walter Rehm distinguishes five kinds of notes: The first group gives the source of a quotation, whereby Jean Paul is showing off his vast knowledge of peculiar facts and data; the second group explains hints and allusions, thus destroying the illusion and somehow dampening the reader by showing him his ignorance; the third group comments on the action, thus stimulating a conversation between the reader and the author; the fourth group represents translations of foreign quotations, which are sometimes humorous or embarrassing because they destroy the mood of climactic or poetic passages; and the fifth group consists of aphorisms taken from Jean Paul's collection of about four thousand maxims which he jotted down when the occasion arose.

A rough survey of the footnotes appearing at the bottom of the pages in *Flegeljahre* shows that half of them belong to the second group and of these only 20 per cent are needed for an understanding of the text. One third of the footnotes refer to obscure sources which are of no importance to us. The few translations, about 5 per cent, are similarly superfluous. Only the third group (about 10 per cent of the total) is actually humorous. When Raphaela, Neupeter's sentimental daughter, speaks in flowery metaphors about the effect of music on her mind, "all the imprisoned tears of my heart will flow . . . tears will water the flowers of joy," [8] the footnote informs us that she took this sentence from Jean Paul's *Hesperus*. This note makes us smile because the idea of an imaginary character reading Jean

101

Paul's book, which is part of the real world, gives us the feeling of sitting in a swing. We participate in Jean Paul's playing with the two worlds of imagination and of reality, swinging from one realm to the other, without staying in either—the very sensation he wants us to experience. Rehm's fifth category, the aphorisms referring to human behavior in general, is not represented in *The Twins*: they have been embodied in the story, underlining the experience or the thoughts of the characters in the novel. In general, then, we may say that although the *basso continuo* of the accompanying footnotes still exists, it has become toned down to the point of inaudibility

III *The Unity of the Story*

Another clue to Jean Paul's intention of attaining classical form is the way in which the novel is divided into volumes and chapters. A comparison between earlier versions and the final text of *The Twins* demonstrates his effort to abandon his capricious and perplexing handling of divisions and subdivisions, giving clarity to the structure and stressing the natural pauses expected by the reader. The chapters of this novel are short; only five of the sixty-four "Numbers" exceed ten pages, whereas the remaining fifty-nine span four to six pages on the average.

In the final version of *The Twins* there is a tendency to combine short chapters, and to have a caesura when a new period of time begins, or when a new character is introduced. Originally Number Five ended after the description of Walt's and Vult's early childhood, and Number Six began with the display of the twin brothers' aptitude for their future careers: Walt to the ministry, and Vult to the law. Subsequently, Jean Paul combined the two Numbers of the pre-history, this part being told by Schomaker, who brings Walt's story up to the day before his law examination. The next chapter, "Quod Deus Vultiana," is told by Vult himself, who gives a summary of his own life after his running away from home—a story unknown to Schomaker which, logically, concentrates on Vult himself. Thus the exposition consists of two clearly separated parts, Walt's youth, and Vult's youth, the former presented by the teacher, the latter by Vult himself from the moment at which he leaves the supervision of his teacher.

A similar approach is taken in Number Seven. Vult is on his way to Elterlein, his native village, from which he had run away ten years ago. After two pages describing his journey home, Jean Paul originally began a new chapter with Vult's entry into Elterlein. In the final version, Number Seven continues to the moment when Vult stands in front of his parents' house, in which Walt is having his examination. This is a more natural break dramatically, bringing the reader into the presence of the story-teller ("Erzählergegenwart") at the point where the actual story begins.

A different reason for a change can be noted in Number Fourteen, "The Magic Night," the first night which the twin brothers spend together after the recognition scene in a churchyard. The scene is rather romantic; and since one wall of Walt's room in the "Inn to the Inn" is missing, the brothers are not really inside and can experience nature as if they were outdoors. Walt urges Vult to watch the enchanting night around them.

The bat, like the tropical bird of beautiful eastern lands, skimmed above their heads, announcing fair weather on the morrow; and on the rose hedges crept the sparkles of the glow-worm: The distant village clocks and the lowing of the herds upon the hills sounded like a lovely echo from ancient time. They needed not, although so late, not even in the thickets a light, for by the reflection of the western sky they saw distinctly the heads of the reapers above the high summer grain. The twilight spread far and broad from the west, with the slender silver crown of the moon upon its head, while at the back of the house crept on unseen, the great deep night from the north. Even at midnight, there was a tender glow in the west, like the color of the apple blossom, and the lightning, faintly flashing from the east, played upon its delicate red. The surrounding birch trees shed their perfume upon the heads of the brothers, and the haycocks their fragrance from the meadow. Many stars peered out in the twilight, and lent wings to their souls.[9]

After this poetic description of the scenery, Walt asks his brother: "Why do you look at me so, dear Vult?"—"I am thinking of past times," Vult replies, "when we used to beat each other. The battle pieces hang like family pictures in my memory." This answer, cooling off Walt and the reader like a cold shower after "a steambath of emotion," [10] is absolutely necessary according to Jean Paul's distribution of sentimentality and realism;

for he will not allow his readers to be completely carried away by their feelings and always pulls us back to this earth. This is his reason for placing the memory of the youthful row at this highly sentimental moment in Number Fourteen, taking it away from Number Six, "Quod Deus Vultiana," where it had served as a pivotal anecdote of the twin brothers' youth, showing Vult as the strong, aggressive, ruthless boy who could, nevertheless, hardly ever win a fistfight with his elastic, quick, and hotheaded brother. This final image of their characters and relationship had to be sacrificed, although it was an impressive end to the "Vultiana" chapter. But the "cold shower" in Number Fourteen was apparently more important for Jean Paul than a logically and esthetically perfect conclusion to the earlier chapter.

Number Nineteen introduces Walt as a notary public. During the preceding Numbers we accompanied him from day to day, not a single one being left out between May 18 and June 20. Eduard Berend feels that the second volume should begin with this Number instead of Number Eighteen because, from Number Nineteen on, the sequence of time is interrupted, and there are days and weeks which are unaccounted for. The natural caesura between these two chapters must have been felt by Jean Paul as well, because he gives more weight to Number Eighteen by adding two important letters. These letters, written by Vult, refer to Walt's admiration for Jonathan von Klothar, a brilliant, proud, cold-hearted young nobleman who dislikes Walt's attempts to approach him and flatly rejects his love when he learns that Walt does not belong to his social class, although he admits that nobody has ever been able to understand him quite as well.

Vult is jealous and disappointed that his friendship does not suffice to Walt; he suffers and knows that he will torture Walt with his jealousy, his sullen spirit, and his "esprit de dépit d'amour." [11] All this was taken from the end of the twenty-first chapter and placed at the end of the eighteenth, thus preparing the mood for the second volume, which relates Walt's attempts to win Klothar's friendship. The question of why the second volume begins with Number Eighteen, even though Jean Paul stresses Number Nineteen as a new beginning after loading the end of Number Eighteen with epic premonitions, can only be answered with a guess: perhaps, unconsciously for Jean Paul, the main character is not Walt but Vult, whose suffering and jealousy begin in Number Eighteen, with Walt being in ecstasies over the "blue young man" (Klothar dressed in blue).

In the second volume, the changes in the division of the chapters follow a new pattern: In the first version Jean Paul usually broke off after a climax, in order to let it take full effect. Now he seems to stress continuity and the even stream of the narrative and slightly levels the feelings and moods of his hero and his readers. Walt's letter to Goldine, a young girl living in his parents' house, (translated by Longfellow in 1843 as "Summertime in Germany"), stood at the end of Number Nineteen, so that nothing should detract from the impression of this poem written in prose. In the final version, five more pages follow. We see Walt run into Klothar's park, where he writes two poems without meter or rhyme—his so-called polymeter. He then is called to the Polish General Zablonski, the father of Wina, the girl he has adored since his childhood. We hear that she is engaged to Klothar, and refuses to convert from Catholicism to Protestantism (Klothar being a Lutheran). By the end of the chapter, "Summertime" is altogether forgotten. Apparently Jean Paul felt that, in spite of its beauty, it was a poetic digression on which our attention should not be focused for too long.

Number Twenty-five is the culminating point of the second volume: at a flute concert given by Vult, Walt sees Wina for the first time. She had visited him once as a child, when he had the measles and could not see her. Originally, Jean Paul described the concert in two chapters, using the intermission as a break and concluding the first with some satirical remarks on the importance of these "vacations from listening," of the "minutes for speaking" which are absolutely necessary for the audience because, like canaries, people are inspired by music to talk; and besides, it is important that people consume something at a concert, be it beer, or tea, or cake. This satire on the audience originally filled the last page of Number Twenty-five. The next chapter began with a realistic description of Wina's appearance by Passvogel, one of the disappointed heirs, followed by Walt's revelation of his eternal love for Wina: "This will be thy first love, thy last, thy only love! suffer what thou wilt . . . he said to himself, considering himself a happy man, . . . to whom, instead of the hundred altars where lie the ashes of love and beauty, the phoenix bird himself, with outstretched golden wings, floats suddenly and from afar before him!" [12]

The combining of these two chapters into one is certainly an improvement over the first version. The climax of a chapter should never be at the beginning because the effect on the reader is stronger when he is led toward it in a crescendo or by means of a contrast like, in this case, the satirical notes about the audience.

One final example of Jean Paul's effective chapter revisions will be taken from the end of the second volume. Again Jean .Paul combines two Numbers so that the last chapter of the volume receives more weight and greater emphasis. After Klothar learns that Walt, in the costume of a nobleman, has been his guest and has successfully deceived him by hiding his low social rank, he offends Walt by attributing to him a base motive for the charade and leaves hastily. This was the end of Number Thirty-two; and the following chapter, the last of the second volume, showed the brothers' reconciliation, bringing the Walt–Vult action to the foreground of the novel. The break between the two chapters might have put a stronger accent on the moving scene of reconciliation between Walt and Vult if it had not been too short (four pages); but it is now better balanced by the first part of the chapter, where Walt and Vult pay their first and last unhappy visit to Klothar.

It is customary to say (and the author says so himself) that Jean Paul is incapable of telling a story and that, in this novel, e.g., the main action—Van der Kabel's last will—is pushed aside by secondary actions, like Walt's unsuccessful attempt to win Klothar's friendship, or the relationship between Walt and Vult, and their love for Wina.[13] It is true that the reader forgets about the plot because he is fascinated by the inner action shown in the development of the characters and the description of their surroundings. However, there is the skeleton of an action, with several strands carefully distributed and used to support the description of that inner life which is most important to Jean Paul.

The first volume, besides giving us the essential points of the pre-history, develops two principal strands: the action initiated by Van der Kabel's last will, and the friendship between Walt and Vult. With the appearance of Klothar, "the Blue Horseman," a conflict (the third strand) comes into existence; for Walt's love for Klothar will mortally wound Vult and destroy the brothers' friendship.

The second volume confirms our premonition. Walt's attempts to win Klothar's friendship form the main contents of this volume; and the friendship between Walt and Vult suffers from Vult's jealousy until, at the end, Klothar leaves and Walt and Vult are reunited. A fourth strand, Walt's love for Wina, then becomes apparent. This development creates new tension because Wina is Klothar's fiancée. The last three strands—Walt–Vult, Walt–Klothar, Walt–Wina—are so closely interwoven that they cannot be separated, whereas the originally intended plot provided by Van der Kabel's last will, is only loosely added to them, e.g., when Walt is active as notary public for one month or tunes pianos for one day or lives for one week in the house of one of the heirs—all the fulfillment of three of the sixteen stipulations.

At the end of the second volume, Walt has unwittingly caused a break between Wina and Klothar, and Vult, perhaps more willingly, has caused the separation of Walt and Klothar, so that we are left with only two strands: Walt–Vult and Walt–Wina. This second action fills the third volume, in which Vult serves as an unconscious catalyst, not knowing with whom Walt is in love. At the end of the volume, "F.R." (Friedrich Richter, the historian of the events in Walt's life, according to Mr. Van der Kabel's will) enumerates all the possible complications that might occur in the following volumes: "O reviewers! reviewers! —if it were my own story, how happily would I invent incidents, change them freely and confuse them. If I added, e.g., a narrow battlefield—a revenant in Schlegel's style of the Euripidean Ion . . . the chains of a lunatic asylum, even the inmates— some painters and their pieces—and the hangman and everything." [14] Even without these romantic complications enough trouble lies ahead: Walt and Wina have to fight for their love, Vult causes difficulties, the disappointed heirs undermine Walt's future, and Klothar may return to marry Wina. In Jean Paul's own words: "Walt tries to remain infinitely good and willing and a delicate Lamb of the Lord; but he is supposed to become a sheep, a buck, when his wool is sheared, when the butcher knives will be used—slings, flames, enemies, friends, heavens, hells wherever one turns! . . ." [15]

In the fourth volume, only Walt's love for Wina figures, but it is accompanied by a new strand of action, Vult's love for Wina. When Wina decides for Walt and against Vult, the latter leaves forever. The novel has no end. Walt is unchanged, since neither Vult nor life has transformed him, and only three of the sixteen stipulations of the will have been fulfilled. Jokingly, "F.R." admits that the only thing he can offer is his pity to the world and to Mr. Cotta, his publisher, who is compelled by his conscience to publish this fragment. Again, Jean Paul ridicules the average reader who is only interested in a plot, in the surface of events. However, in comparison with his earlier novels, Jean Paul does not confuse us any more than is absolutely necessary, and then only to make us aware of what is important to the author himself.

We have been able to prove that in *The Twins* there is a skeleton of a plot, with several strands of action being clearly distinguished by a careful distribution through four volumes and sixty-four Numbers. The pre-history fills the first volume, with some missing facts supplied later in the second volume. Jean Paul uses predominantly third-person narrative. Only rarely does he jump to the first person, with the consequent interruption of time and action. If there are digressions, they are used, indirectly, to characterize Walt and Vult or form an ironic contrast to a scene full of romantic feeling and poetic description.

Jean Paul stretches time more often than he telescopes it, but this is the privilege of the epic author; it is up to him to stress certain moments that are more important than others. The perspective of the narrator is, for the most part, identical with that of Walt, the protagonist. There are two exceptions, however, when "JPFR" (Jean Paul Friedrich Richter) reports directly to the city council of Hasslau. These are rare occasions when Jean Paul can play with us in his favorite way and make fun of his readers, his critics, and his publisher, squeezing his famous prologues, interludes, and epilogues into a few chapters.

But apart from these exceptional digressions, Jean Paul guides his reader with the help of epic premonitions, thereby building bridges and gangways. We are, e.g., allowed to read Vult's letter to Walt with the description of Klothar's character, which Walt must not open until later. Therefore, we are less surprised than Walt when Klothar displays his true character. He is only theoretically capable of renouncing the rights of his noble birth; in reality he cannot even allow an educated person like Walt to approach him as a loving human being, for the sole reason that Walt is not nobly born. The setting for this revealing scene is carefully prepared by Jean Paul some chapters before, when Walt visits Klothar's park for the first time. We accompany him to a place with a rock and a waterfall on one side and the marble statue of a Vestal on the other. We are not surprised that, in the decisive conversation when Klothar and Walt stand at the same place, the former has to shout because of the waterfall; and we smile, in spite of Walt's despair, when we see the Vestal looking down upon him as if he were her husband.

Jean Paul calls the epic writer's ability to build bridges to the past and future a historical talent. This is Vult's gift in the novel; he bursts with impatience when Walt's reports do not progress because he "sees only one fact at a time and paints and decorates it incessantly." [16] In the preceding chapter, the narrator has informed us that history does not proceed systematically: "Over the whole historical picture gallery of the world, the greatest clouds change into less, and the smallest become greater . . . and the Invisible God alone can evolve the serious and true from the eternal play of life and history." [17] This shows us that Jean Paul was well aware of what the average reader expects of an author. The author, who is Vult as well as Walt, uses Vult's historical talent only to the extent that we are not confused and can recognize the main elements of the story.

On the whole, Jean Paul is primarily interested in the presentation of the inner life; Nature, e.g., plays a part only when it expresses what Man cannot say, so that the external and the internal are not antitheses, the external detail being a manifestation of the protagonist's inner state.[18] When Walt wanders aimlessly, experiencing the delight of a spring day although it is September, when his restlessness and the coming of a thunderstorm coincide on the second day, when he reaches the climax of his journey and feels a profound admiration for God's splendor as it is manifested in the presence of Wina and the overwhelming beauty of a mountain waterfall changed into a bridge of fire by the rising sun, it is hard to say whether the external or the internal predominates. Both serve the same purpose: to stress the emotional aspects, so that the external world is presented only through the feeling of the individual and as a reflection of consciousness.

The unity of the story is sustained by the author's subjective involvement; for Jean Paul is seeking self-knowledge by presenting the opposing elements of his own character in the figures of the twin brothers. In his earlier novels, such as *Siebenkäs*, he created characters like Siebenkäs, Leibgeber and Lenette, whom we take to be people of this world; people we have met, loved, pitied, admired, and who are as real, or more so, than our friends of flesh and blood. Walt and Wina, however, cannot compare with real beings. Walt seems rather to have come out of a fairy tale—a pure, innocent dreamer who is not aware of reality and finally wins the princess. We cannot compare him to Parzival or Simplizissimus, both of whom develop into mature men, whereas Walt remains unchanged from the first to the fourth volume. He would, for that matter, be the same at the end of the thirtieth volume, had Jean Paul ever written it.

Jean Paul presents his views on the creation of a genuine character in his *Introduction to Esthetics*. Walt is an example of the mixed character, having an overwhelming quantity of love combined with some weaknesses;[19] Wina, being a woman and having, therefore, according to Jean Paul, less individuality, is best suited to represent an ethical ideal.[20] All characters must be representatives of a class or genus, creating a mythology of souls, just as Hamlet is the father of all Werthers.[21] But Walt and Wina have no astronomical "latitude or altitude"[22]—they are always shown at their best. Only Vult knows both height and depth of passion, feeling, and action and, therefore, impresses us as a real person. We must not forget that the main character of *The Twins* is Jean Paul himself, not the historic person who lived from 1763 to 1825, but rather his "ideal ego of the poetic ego,"[23] which he investigates without ever coming to a conclusion.

IV *Integrated Descriptions*

More important than this goal is Jean Paul's style, not *what* is presented, but *how* it is presented by means of metaphors, dreams, and stream of consciousness, as counterbalanced by bitter satire, wit, irony, and reflections upon reflections. In a metaphorical style that grows more and more picturesque and impressive, Jean Paul gives us descriptions of such perfection that we will never forget them. In the second volume, for example, we celebrate Peter Neupeter's birthday in a typical nouveau-riche scene where every detail is original and significant. This description is an indirect characterization of Walt integrated with the progressing action. At the same time, however, Jean Paul has a chance to exhibit his vast knowledge and his wisdom.

The rich merchant Neupeter has not sent a written invitation to Walt because, in his opinion, he would not add anything to the glamor of the occasion, whereas Glantz, the superintendent of churches, does, and even more so, Klothar, who is a nobleman. Walt does not feel hurt; he does not want to be distinguished. Looking through the handrails, he watches the arriving guests from the top floor, where he lives, and slips into the festive rooms of the second floor together with a larger group of latecomers. The chairs of the banquet room, normally hidden by slipcovers, have taken off "their caps for each derrière," the protecting linen rugs are removed, and the golden doorknobs are freed from their paper wrappings. In the dining room, before the serving of the soup, Neupeter's daughters decorate their father with flower garlands; a printed poem is distributed among the guests, of which the host is handed a guilded copy; the orchestra intones the tune, and all those present, Neupeter himself included, sing the poem in his honor, like saying a particularly lengthy grace.

The tableware—china, silver, golden knives for fruit—, and the elaborate meal—with artichokes, smoked salmon, the Mainz ham, baked dishes and sweets—display the glamor of the house. After a lively conversation about politics, theology, and philosophy (carried on aggressively on Klothar's and enthusiastically on Walt's side), the company moves into Neupeter's park, which also displays the merchant's wealth, with marble statues of children and a Hercules among flowers—all of them very expensive, as Neupeter points out. The center of attraction is a lake with an island, on which the late Christhelf Neupeter stands "hewn in stone with the dress he wore upon the Bourse translated into marble, with his wig and the petrified wrinkles in his worsted stockings and his coat-skirts. . . . [This appearance] gave no one even the idea that the old merchant could ever have been undraped." [24]

A bridge painted in rainbow colors leads to a wooden pyramid hanging partly over the water, into which Klothar happily disappears after having learned from Neupeter that this structure is especially useful after heavy drinking. Neupeter is as proud of this invention as of his daughter's "sentimental tablets hanging from the trees. Like a physician's prescription on a glass of medicine they told in what doses, in what spoons, and at what hours beautiful nature should be taken" (I, 145).

Another unforgettable description in *The Twins* is that of Walt's three-day trip to the Rosana Valley, of which the trip of Eichendorff's "Taugenichts" seems only to be a weak imitation. Early in the morning Walt leaves, stops under the four wooden arms of a signpost, carefully avoids looking up, so that he cannot read the names of the villages which, in any case, the rain has practically obliterated.

His main object was not to know the name of any town, nor even of the villages. He hoped thus, without any decided aim, and a sort of imaginary uncertainty, to wind about among the pleasure-grounds and flowerbeds of wayfaring and see only what should arise before him at every new step; to pray in every green, gold-waving grove; in every little hamlet to ask its name, and secretly to exult in his knowledge. With such measures, he hoped that even in a small compass of country he might, perhaps, find country houses, irregular gardens, a diminutive Switzerland; and that his imagination might fill it with mountain castles, and beautiful eyes within them looking down upon him; chapels with pilgrims; and eyes raised in prayers: accidents, and romantic adventures were sown in numbers over his journey, such as he could never, in sober reality, expect. Infinite good! in thy clear blue heaven, he prayed in his exquisite delight, this once let not my excessive joy be the omen of disappointment! (I, 48-49).

He is so happy that he loves even dogs and shakes "paws" with them. Three little girls, triplets, so arouse his enthusiasm that he wants to be omnipotent in order to be able to create a tiny little world for little children who would never grow up. Jean Paul, the happy father of three children, knew from experience what delight it is to watch children play in their paradise of innocence. Walt sings while he is walking ahead.

How beautiful it is in these pillared halls of nature, the living green above and beneath, an eternal succession of infinite life. . . . He looked at a flock of silent nightingales preparing for their nightly annual flight. "Where do you fly with your sweet spring complaint? Seek you the myrtle for love? Seek you the laurel for song? Do you desire to meet eternal spring and ever golden stars? Ah! Fly where there are no storms beneath the clouds, and sing in the fairest lands; but return again in our spring, and sing to the thirsting heart the longing strain of *Heimweh* for its own celestial country. Trees and flowers! Ye bow yourselves hither and thither as though you were living, and would speak to our hearts. I love you as though I were myself a flower, with its blossoms. Ah! once I lived a higher life . . ." (I, 60-61).

When Walt hears a flute player in the valley, he lies down in the grass near a brook. "He loved not one or another living being, but *all* life itself, not merely the prospect, the grass, the woods, the clouds and the golden insect, he bent low to observe the smallest earthworms, their bread-trees and their pleasure-gardens. He would pause in the midst of writing his poems, if a weak and spotted insect was working his way over the smooth surface of the paper, lest he should crush or disturb him. Ach Gott! he said, how can any one destroy life, if he only look upon it rightly, for a single moment" (I, 61–62). The description becomes an echo of his feelings, and the stream of consciousness turns into a stream of impressions formulated in meter and rhymeless verse, in ecstatic stanzas: "Wherefore dost thou weep? What has thou lost? Who is dead for you? Ah! I have lost nothing. For me no one is dead. Oh, suffer me to weep for I have never yet loved!" (I, 66).

A last idyll, the nucleus, or, in Friedrich Gundolf's words, the breeding cell of the novel, is constituted by the double life of the twin brothers sharing the same nest, or double cage, like two birds. Some privacy is guaranteed by a partition of painted material, a prop borrowed from the theater and dividing the room in two parts. On Walt's side, it shows a palace, on Vult's side an Arcadian village. A window of the painted palace allows the twins to speak to each other. Even without the window, however, they can talk easily through wall and town, so that the physical separation will not entail a spiritual one. Both twins are in a gentle mood after their reconciliation at the end of the second volume, "for it was easy, if the wolf in the heart was killed, to be outwardly soft lambs" (II, 204). The conversations carried on between the brothers show no signs of sentimentality. They veil their innermost feelings in generalizations like "The highest love knows no middle ground. It is only Yes or No! It can dwell in no purgatory. It makes a heaven or hell. And it has this misfortune, that the feelings and proclivities to which it gives birth, are in themselves purgatory, the portresses of heaven or hell" (II, 205).

They work steadily all day long, trying to finish their joint novel. Towards four o'clock they have tea—quite an experience for Walt who, until now, has taken tea only after a laxative. The twins' endless discussions center about the necessity of their togetherness, about winter as a creative season, about the plot of the novel, its entanglements and disentanglements, and, above all, about their dealings with publishing houses. This is their most exciting parlor game: the mailing of the unfinished manuscript, accompanying it, in thought, on its way to Leipzig; waiting for the answer; their wrath and despair when the manuscript is returned; and Vult's sarcastic letters to the publishers, which he mails without postage.

After tea the brothers go for a walk to get some fresh air, Walt always keen to observe people as future material for his novel. They spend the evening at home, Vult playing the flute, and Walt dreaming happily during this "flute playing dusk of the nightingale" (II, 214), which inspires him to create new polymeters. However, this idyll cannot last, since Vult in spite of his misanthropy is unstable and somewhat dependent on a larger audience. After two evenings with Walt, he goes out at night, sits around in coffee houses, angry with himself and his company, but finally getting used to them and to their boring conversation. He spends the morning with Walt, who has found a new subject for their conversation: their common childhood memories, which he recounts lovingly to a sardonic accompaniment by Vult.

V *Images of Motion and Temporal Confusion*

The idyll of the twin brothers' common life is never boring because Jean Paul has created an inner tension that runs like a *basso continuo* under the idyllic surface: both of them love Wina without knowing about each other's infatuation. The reader can easily guess that this idyll will break up as soon as Vult finds out about Walt's love for Wina; and Jean Paul augments this tension in a dreamlike scene enacted during a late evening when

Wina, her friend Raphaela, and the latter's sister meet in Neupeter's park to do some ice skating on the lake with the pyramid, which we know so well from Neupeter's birthday party. This time the mood is completely different. We encounter no sarcastic comment, no unpoetic gesture. It is Walt's dream world come to life when the three young girls and Vult fly over the ice, weightless, unreal, matched by Walt who ventures a few steps away from the bank of the lake in order to be closer to Wina. A conversation is going on, short questions are asked, significant answers given, rhythmically interrupted by the approaching and gliding away of the ice skaters. The scene proceeds through a short rococo-like play with words between Vult and Raphaela's sister, and Vult's serious attempt to surround Wina with his magic circles, to a dialogue between Wina and Walt, who gives her the poem and the music she had asked the brothers to prepare for Raphaela's birthday. Above all, it is Walt's complete happiness at Vult's flute-playing as the leader of the chorus which gives music of the nine spheres to the heavenly bodies on the ice.

. . . The other [Vult] flew off, and like the choral leader of the music of the spheres, the heavenly orbs seemed to float before and after him on the ice. . . . If the art of music so powerfully penetrates the heart with its poetry, in the common festivals of the world, the soul is completely moved by it in the open air, and in a man like Walt, it inspires, instead of earthly passions, only heavenly emotions, such as filled the shore with quiet thanksgivings; and while his songs of joy echoed around the lake, the world of his heart, as often as the sound of the flute penetrated it, was re-created and sanctified anew. He collected all the joy of others, like warm beams into the burning point of his concentrated soul. . . . The while, shining stars seemed suspended, like sporting nightingales, from heaven; and the moon wove its consecrated beams together into Wina's form (II, 259).

A similar image of motion, occasioned by the dancers who are accompanied by music, appears at the end of the fourth volume, in the chapter entitled "The Dance of the Masks." Here the dreamlike atmosphere is heightened by the dancers' masks. "Like spirits from distant western worlds, they looked at each other; and as stars are made visible by the eclipse of the sun, thus souls, however remote, behind these masks, could see, and understand each other" (II, 288). Although Walt is a poor dancer, he feels transformed by the music.

115

In the midst of the dance, he endeavored to prove to Wina that through the act of dancing the body might become music; that man might form wings, and soar, even in his life; that two souls might themselves be alone, in absolute solitude, even in the midst of a multitude; and, like certain heavenly bodies surrounded by an atmosphere of their own, revolve only around the axis of each other; that those only who love should dance, so that in the symmetrical grace of this art the harmony of their souls might have room to play. . . . A ball *en masque* is perhaps the most elevated theme that *humorous* poetry can venture to sport with. In the view of the poet, all ranks and all periods are equal, and the outward only the garment, where the inside is happiness and splendor; thus here, where the oldest fashions and customs have revived, and wander around, mingling with the latest and the youngest, here humanity and life itself have become poetry . . . All that never before were brought together . . . are rounded in one easy, joyful circle; and the circle moves splendidly to the measure of music; for music is the climate of the soul, as this masquerade is the theatre of the body. *One* only stands here serious, undisguised, unmasked, and regulates the cheerful confusion (II, 288).

Wina responds hastily, in a low voice, by saying that Walt's ideas are poetry: "Your views are in themselves poetry; but to a being of a more exalted nature, the history of humanity may appear, indeed, only the long disguise of a masquerade" (II, 290).

Vult interrupts their metaphysical dialogue, and now we enter the enchanting, floating, and flying world of Jean Paul. Unrecognizable in Walt's costume, imitating Walt's voice and adopting his manner, Vult dances with Wina, whose costume is that of a nun. They touch hands, cross each other; and "towards the end of the dance, Vult, in crossing hands, in leading up or down, allows many Polish words, as it were the breath of a language, to escape him" (II, 295). Vult utters Polish words because this is Wina's mother tongue.

Like butterflies, wandering over the sea, from a remote island, or like the rare and distant song of the lark on a late autumnal day, were these sounds to Wina. . . . As the second part of the music rose in its deep waves of harmony into that voluptuous overfulness of sound, which, like all adagios, powerfully moves the inmost soul; and the secret wishes of the heart rise from the sea of waves, and the waltzers and the lights whirl confusedly together, and the wide sound and the tumult cause the disguised masks to shrink deeper into their disguises; Vult, in his flight, said softly, but in Polish, "Protected by the deep foliage of flower-leaves, happiness rushes and revolves around us—wherefore am I the only one for whom it perpetually dies? Why is there, for me, neither heaven nor earth? Nun! Thou art both! In thee is all my heaven!" (II, 296-97).

Wina is misled by Vult's appearance and confused by the whirling of the dance that allows only a brief contact, separating the partners immediately, heading each dancer his own prescribed way before they are allowed to meet again for a moment. She feels isolated because none of the other masks is familiar to her after her friend Raphaela has left with her partner. Vult's urgent question whether Wina will change Gottwalt, God May Lead, into a Gottverlassner, Left Alone By God, is answered by her silence, which Vult interprets correctly as "no." This is a negative declaration of love for Walt, whom she believes to be her partner.

This unusual declaration of love, a silent negation meaning "no, I shall not make you unhappy" instead of a simple "yes, I love you," leaves the reader somewhat dizzy because he has to do an about-face and pursue his thinking in the opposite direction. This stylistic device of pulling the ground from under our feet so that we stumble and almost forget to breathe before we can pull ourselves together and return to the action, is called "romantic" by Jean Paul (II, 311). He does it in order to confuse us.

Wina's father shows Walt a portrait in which Wina is shown bending down with a motherly gesture to a little daughter, her image, though different from her in age. We are as confused as Walt, since we think we know that she has no child. The general wants Walt to understand that Wina is represented twice in the painting, which will be a gift to Wina's mother, of whom no portrait exists. Since Wina looks exactly like her mother at Wina's age, the artist had only to paint Wina twice as "Bild and Urbild" (II, 377), i.e., as portrait and original image. Wina's mother will get the impression that she sat for this portrait at a distance of forty miles. Thus "romantic" confusion is created for two characters in the novel (Walt and Wina's mother) as well as for the reader.

In moments of great happiness, Walt refrains from writing a poem because it seems to him that he himself was transformed into a poem, and that "he bowed easily to the rhythm of an unknown enchanted poet" (II, 310). Meals taken at an unusual time, dressing for an occasion at night while other people undress to go to bed, confuse Walt, his body as well as his mind, and throw him out of his tracks. From such experiences Jean Paul deduces that this may be a reason why soldiers, who live long enough outside the usual order, feel that war is "romantic."

In the second volume of the novel, Vult sends a letter to Walt which the latter is not supposed to read but is to return after having put his seal on it. The same letter is handed over to Walt a second time in the fourth volume. Walt does not immediately recognize it; he takes it for a newly written letter, but Vult shows him the original date, "which we read earlier than Walt or rather later" (II, 203). We are to understand that Walt reads the letter in the fourth volume while we read it in the second—however, only after the publication of the novel.

The treatment of time is certainly confusing; and the intermingling of reality and the imaginary world contributes to the "romantic" mood. A new confusion of writer and reader is created when Vult writes in his diary that he admits "to his gentle reader, to good Vult. . ." who writes *and* reads his own diary. He adds: "To me, writing is so indifferent, O Vult!" (II, 208). Jean Paul symbolizes his twisting and turning upside down of situations and ideas in the image of flying. During the dance Walt explains to Wina that they are transformed into music, and that they are flying while life stands still. The same image recurs in Walt's dream, where he sees a river standing still while the ocean moves along the banks of the river: "Then there passed through the sea a stream bearing the form of Venus. It paused, and the sea closed about the beautiful form" (II, 415). In a witty mood, Jean Paul found a perfect metaphor for the twisting of things: a mask at the ball was a shoe that wore itself.

There are many examples of this kind to be found in *The Twins*, all of them affecting us in such a way that we seem to be floating in the air on a swing, one of Jean Paul's favorite occupations. However, this swinging is not meant to put us to sleep like the rocking of a cradle. If we want to enjoy the sensation we must be made awake, reveling in the motion, flying *with* him, hanging on to every word. Perhaps his insistence on total involvement is one of the reasons why Jean Paul does not have too many readers.

VI Leitmotifs, Chapter Headings, and Maxims

Another impressive stylistic device is Jean Paul's use of the leitmotif. One of Wina's leitmotifs is the flower auricula, which is mentioned for the first time when she visits Walt as a child. He is very ill, almost blind, and Wina pities him so much that she throws all her auriculas on his bed, so that he is intoxicated by their freshness and fragrance. In the portrait which shows her as her mother and as a child, the little girl holds an auricula in one hand and places a butterfly on it with the other. A bouquet of auriculas is in Wina's hand during the masquerade. Auriculas are early spring flowers that grow high up in the mountains. Like most Alpine flowers, they are small, but their color is intense—a golden yellow—and their fragrance delicate and fresh. All these qualities combined create the image of purity, modesty, and intensity, with the added suggestion of closeness to heaven. This leitmotif characterizes Wina in an indirect way through emotion—a technique which is discussed by Jean Paul in his *Introduction to Esthetics* (§79).

Another striking leitmotif used for characterization and as a catalyst of the action are the wooden boards with poetic inscriptions hanging from Neupeter's trees—one of Roberta's fancy ideas. We see them for the first time on Neupeter's birthday when they enhance the heavy, tasteless atmosphere of the home of a nouveau riche who interprets Raphaela's sentimentality as a genuine understanding of literature. We see the same boards when they arouse Vult's wrath in the moonlit night after the ice-skating. Vult prefers to walk in the dark part of the park, so that he is not forced to read about feelings nailed on trees, because he hates "that turning out, and exposing of inward emotion as if man could be reversed like a polypus, and the inside become the outside" (II, 262). Here the boards are used to characterize Vult, who hates any display of feelings and is impatient with the poor taste of less sensitive people.

Walt likes the inscriptions; he even uses one of them in the poem which Wina will sing on the morning of Roberta's birthday: "Dost thou dream who loves you?" (II, 271). Vult quotes this line when he hurries, with Wina, to the place where they are supposed to start their morning concert. Vult stops for a moment under the tree that is decorated with this line. He sings the text, which he purposely set to music for the occasion: "Dost thou dream who loves you?" This devious, subtle way of declaring his love characterizes Vult and, at the same time, furthers the action: Vult's indirect question whether Wina knows about his love will call forth her decision for or against him.

This use of leitmotifs, together with other stylistic devices, proves that Jean Paul departed radically from his original model, Sterne's *Tristram Shandy*, to a more classical, carefully planned and structured form of the novel. We still recognize the young Jean Paul, the admirer of Sterne, in some of the digressions, and more fully in the titles of the "Numbers" which carry the strange names of the different pieces in Van der Kabel's cabinet of minerals. Only in some rare instances do they have a meaning for the chapter they are heading. Number Thirty is called "Misspickels aus Sachsen," meaning "White Pebbles from Saxony" (II, 298). "Misspickel," however, reminds the German reader of mixed pickles, something that is sharp and spicy. According to Herman Meyer, "Misspickel" refers to poisonous arsenical pyrites, and thus alludes to Vult's sharp criticism of others and to his sulkiness.[25] The subtitle, "Discussion on Nobility," points to the subject of the chapter: a satire on the nobility voiced by Vult. This, however, is not the only or even the principal topic of the chapter, which describes Vult's visit to his home town where, for the first time, he meets Wina, who inspires him to write a polymetric poem in Walt's style. This is the turning point of the Walt-Vult story. It will bring about the end of the twin brothers' common life and, with it, the end of the novel. Of the twelve pages of this chapter only two fit the title.

Number Thirty-five, "Chrysoprase," describes Walt as rejoicing at Wina's return from her trip, and listening to her singing in the next room: "He was entranced by the beautiful tones" (II, 212). The subtitle, "To Dream—to Sing—to Pray—to Dream," is entirely fitting, as is the softly opaque, delicate milky green of the chrysoprase. "Genuine Noble Garnet—The Fresh Day," Number Forty-six, is also a well-chosen title for the description of the second day of Walt's trip, which ends with a romantic sunset ride on a ferryboat. During the ride, Walt studies Wina's face without her noticing, while she sits in her carriage and he stands within the crowd on the boat. "A Worn-out Fly Catcher" is like a symbol for Flitte, one of Van der Kabel's heirs whose cheerful life and easygoing nature are the subject of Number Fifty-two.

The climax of the last volume, "The Dance of the Masks" (Number Sixty-three), is the ball at which Vult forces Wina to confess whom she loves. This scene reminds the reader of Jean Paul of another climactic scene at the end of *Titan*, where Roquairol seduces Linda, Albano's fiancée, by taking advantage of her night-blindness and the similarity of his and Albano's voices. Recognizing this parallel, the reader of *Flegeljahre* is well prepared for Number Sixty-three as soon as he sees the title, "Titan–Turmalin," turmalin being in most cases pitch black —although the end of the "German" novel *Flegeljahre* is less tragic than that of the "Italian" novel *Titan*.

Most of the remaining titles in *The Twins* are chosen only for their strangeness and their shock value, e.g., Mammoth Bones from Astracan; Berlin Marble with Shining Spots; Sassafras; Congerie of Mouse-Gray Cats' Tails; Polished Stick of Amber; A Worn-out Justice Robe; Lapis Suillus.

In addition to his playful propensity for confusing us occasionally and for misleading us with strange titles, Jean Paul also uses the epigram and maxim to strong effect. These are always highly pertinent; but by their very trenchancy they force us to stop and ponder, thus distracting our attention from the narrative. We know that the poet jotted down these remarks whenever they came to his mind; that he collected them carefully, and that he read and reread them before writing a novel. Eduard Berend is preparing a new collection of these *Thoughts* within the frame of *Jean Pauls Sämtliche Werke*. It would seem superfluous to extract them from *Flegeljahre* after Jean Paul embedded the so carefully in a context. However, they show so much common sense that some examples should be quoted here if we are to be fair to this supposedly sentimental author.

Walt is extremely happy when he can report to his brother on the experiences of his trip because "no adventure, even the worst one, is ever as happily experienced as told" (II, 148). At another time Walt is sad since part of his expected inheritance was lost because of his mistakes as a notary public. But when the day arrives on which he has to face the judgment he remains serene, for "the common miseries of life give us less pain at their birth than during their pregnancy, and the *true* day of sorrow begins ever twenty-four hours sooner than the real one" (II, 148), and "only a man is able to write poetry—to sleep—to read before a turning point in his life, not a woman" (II, 155).

Walt admires his host, Flitte, and praises him immeasurably, although he sees his shortcomings; but he poignantly reminds us that "praise is like air, the only thing a human being can and must swallow incessantly" (II, 155). In spite of his sincere effort to become emotionally indispensable to his brother, Vult has no illusions about the kind of love Walt feels for him: "Innocent as an animal, [Walt] can only love poetically, not some Hans or Kunz, but rather, as in Klothar, the badly painted picture of the saint of his soul's innermost image which he adores on his knees." Or, as in Vult's ironic metaphor, "In art, as under the sun, only hay warms up, not the living flowers" (II, 214–15).

Vult is less poetic but perhaps more profound when he describes mankind's struggle for success in terms of miners scrambling up a ladder. The miner standing higher on the ladder directs his eyes less to the one below him but to the derrière of the one above him. Diametrically opposed to those who struggle for success are those who love, and in their glorified world the giver thanks the receiver: "To *ask* a favor of one who loves is to give more than to receive. But why in love alone is this an exception? Why is there no enlightened world when all human requests would be considered favors; and the asker be thanked, rather than the benefactor?"

VII *Dream Poems*

At the end of the novel, Walt tells his brother about an "artistically arranged" dream, which is generally considered a masterpiece among Jean Paul's dream poems. Dreams play an important part in that author's thinking and writing. Jean Paul wrote several essays on dreams, and there are fourteen dreams in his fictional work, some closely integrated with the plot, others loosely connected or simply added as an afterthought.[26] Max Kommerell points out that Jean Paul clearly distinguishes between dreams that are a repetition of the day's experience and those that seem to give us an insight into our fate before birth and after death, a knowledge, essential and *a priori*, that is apprehended by the soul.[27] In his efforts to render his visions,

Jean Paul mixes the realms of our senses—colors resound, sounds give light. All elements are freed of their form and put together in a new order, so that they remind us of reality, but present a new surrealistic world. In that world, thoughts are more power- ful than laws of physics; with them we can move trees and dis- solve icebergs. Everything changes its original form; only sounds remain unchanged because they seem to be immaterial as com- pared to form and color. The world is turned back into chaos so that it can become one with God, and the discord between God and the created world will be transformed into harmony at the beginning of eternity. Based on his knowledge of Jean Paul's mystical sources, Smeed gives a thorough explanation of the dream by translating the language of the dream vision into the clear abstract language of philosophy. The reader knows exactly what the dream means, whereas Walt himself confesses that he lost the meaning after he woke up. In this dream Walt sees two suns: God says to himself the first word and answers the first word, You and I. God gives the possibility of love to man, but also man gives the possibility of love to God. This is an example of the symbolic language of mysticism which Jean Paul learned indirectly from eighteenth-century pietism, from baroque mys- ticism, and finally directly from Jacob Böhme whose works he read in 1801.[28] The elder Breughel gave him inspiration for the grotesque representation of evil and hell.[29] The struggle between time and eternity followed by a unique moment of mystical in- sight, the *unio mystica*, and afterwards the return to this world, is presented by mystical writers as well as by Jean Paul.

At the beginning of the dream in the *Flegeljahre*, we have a new cosmogony; trees grow out of flowers, clouds out of trees; and flowers break through the clouds. A gray and spotty egg, out of which the universe will be "hatched," swims on the ocean, through which a stream seems to float with the dead Venus, the symbol of that love that wants self-satisfaction instead of *caritas*, meaning love that leads us to God.[30] Stars fall like snow, the sky stays empty until it is covered by the ocean, which piles up in enormous bulges like snakes. Sad human beings enter this world, and the dark night follows them. Thus the created world is hostile, cheerless; and being born is as miserable as dying.

The symbol of the second world is a golden bee that flies slowly and sings gently to a starlet sucking at the latter's white blossoms. But the Manichean struggle is not yet over; and the evil enemy tells the secret legend of the creation:[31] Once upon a time there was an eternal legend that lived in the last corner of the world, longing and yearning. Only through longing can the mystical thinker approach God, who visits the legend in Walt's dream, in order to see whether it is still longing. The dreamer glides through the winged waves of a sky-high ocean. He cannot attain the "true land" where the sun's rays are transformed into music, where golden-green clouds send warm rain, and where liquid light drops from roses and lilies, out of reach for the dreamer who is enclosed by the glassy ocean.

All sleeps in the *true* land . . . love only dreams. Then came a morning star, and kissed a white rose-bud; it opened its cup, and spread its petals to the star; a caressing zephyr hung upon the highest branch of an oak; one of the softest tones came, and kissed the May-flower; it opened its little bell and was borne swiftly upwards. . . . The twilight of the true land awoke again; but all was changed, because the flowers, the stars, and the sounds, all were slumbering children. Every child embraced a child, and the beams of Aurora sounded continually around them.[32]

The climax of the dream duly represents the innocent love of children as the only means of approaching God.[33]

Now the children played among each other *loving*. "Be my flower," said one to another. The other complied and suffered itself to be worn on the breast of the asker. "Be my little star," said another, and it was so. "Be my God." "And thou mine," they said to each other. They did not change but looked at each other with warmer love and vanished, as though dying therein. "Remain with me," the children said to each other, "even if thou must depart." Thus the departing child became first like a soft flush of evening in the distance and then like a faint evening star and receded into the horizon, like a shimmer of moonlight, and, at length, from distance to distance, it was lost in the fading sound of a flute, or the softest note of the nightingale.[34]

The mystic longs to return to the Divine Presence, to be drawn up by the "Allklang," the divine tone that has the power of transforming us completely into a part of eternal Being. But at that moment Walt "is saved by sleep";[35] for man is not allowed to experience fully the final transformation.

Ursula Gauhe, who has investigated Jean Paul's mystical vocabulary,[36] and Eva Baratta, who stresses less the meaning than the formal analysis of Jean Paul's metaphors, take a more esthetic approach.[37] Examining the text word for word, Mrs. Baratta separates the genuine dream vision from Jean Paul's commentary and his allegorical interpretation.[38] Thus the structure of the dream becomes visible: the first part is richer in untrammeled visions than the second, which loses the dream character by changing the attitude of the storyteller from unconscious vision to half-conscious and, finally, conscious allegorical interpretation.[39] The first part is, therefore, richer in grotesque, shocking, and surrealistic images that must be accepted at face value and cannot be explained unequivocally. A comparison with Jean Paul's notes, where he jotted down automatically his dream experiences, shows that this original stream of metaphors is unlyrical and unbalanced. Only after choosing the most impressive images and forming them poetically does Jean Paul attain the dreamlike effect.[40]

Eva Baratta denies that this dream is integrated into the novel, and that it presents any psychological characterization of Walt. She calls it a mystical, metaphysical statement like Kafka's dreams.[41] For Peter Horst Neumann, however, the dream has a strong epic function; it is a compilation of the images dispersed throughout the novel.[42] He sees in Walt's dream the keystone of the work. He also admits that the metaphors are similar to a code, but maintains that they cannot be taken out of the context. In his view, the essence of the novel is once more presented in the dream, but on another level.[43]

The esthetic interpretations of Eva Baratta, Ursula Gauhe, and P. H. Neumann give many insights into Jean Paul's stylistic richness and his overall achievements as a novelist. Jean Paul the poet, in the many dream poems that fill his work, seems peculiarly close to Louis Kampf's ideal of artist as opposed to critic, the artist teaching us to transform regular life into an artistic vision, and to find a symbolic meaning in our experiences.[44]

CHAPTER 7

The Comet

T HE COMET, Jean Paul's last comical novel, unfinished but monumental, offers perhaps the easiest approach to his work for the modern reader. It is a bitter satire ridiculing mankind and was originally planned as an "Encyclopedia of the Burlesque" in the form of an open novel, without plot or continuity, containing only interesting divertissements.[1] The principal action concerns an angel who is trying to find inhabitants for another planet and chooses the characters of Jean Paul's *Comet*. Another theme had topical relevance around 1811 when Jean Paul was writing the book: Goethe wins the jackpot in a lottery and spends all the money to end the monotony of court life in Weimar by engaging Jean Paul's characters.[2] However, Jean Paul abandoned his plan to create a "pantheon of fun" and settled for an "innocent and noble roguery," [3] the story of one fool, Nikolaus Marggraf, who takes a journey with good-natured and egotistical fools and two normal people, his sister and *Kandidat* Richter, the author's voice who, in this case, is not the storyteller, but an actual character within the story.

The story itself is very simple: Marggraf is in search of his father, a prince, whose name he does not even know, and of his beloved, a princess, of whom he caught a glimpse when he was a boy. He later stole her wax bust and hid it in an empty clock case in a loft, where he went often in secret to idolize her. During the journey, the bust sits facing him in his carriage. Marggraf loves her with the same ardor and ecstasy which Gustav felt for Beata, Victor for Klotilde, Albano for Liane, Walt for Wina. But the reader of *The Comet* is not expected to share the lover's ecstasy or Jean Paul's revelry; he is allowed to smile or even laugh at them, and laughter comes more naturally than ecstasies and tears to the modern reader. Even the first readers of *The Comet* in 1820, when Volumes One and Two of the novel were published, and in 1822, when Volume Three was finished, differed from the readers of the late eighteenth century. Instead of members of the nobility, principally young women, Jean Paul now reached students at the universities. Disillusioned by the Restoration, these students saw in him the representative of a future Germany.

Goerres, the editor of the "Volksbücher" turned to Jean Paul, and Friedrich von der Hagen sent him his first edition of the *Nibelungenlied.* When students and professors at Heidelberg University honored him enthusiastically, only the "Landsmann-schaften" objected to it.[4] His new followers loved him for his attack on censorship in the introduction to the first volume, as well as for the Second Section of the third volume, in which *Kandidat* Richter pronounces a sermon on the death of a maid-servant, Regina. Regina had served her master for forty years, and had slavishly carried out his orders. She had never escaped servitude, not even in her dreams. Nor had she ever been invited to a party, but had only prepared them and served at them. She would never have heard dance music if she had not accompanied her mistress home after a ball. All through her life, only her work was respected, not her individuality. She died shortly after having been publicly honored for her faithful services, on which occasion the sympathetic Nikolaus Marggraf decorated her with his watch hanging on a red ribbon. She did not dare to wind it, for fear she might break it. The story is exaggerated and sentimental, but satire and irony are used as sharp, aggressive weapons against Regina's exploiters, an attitude that pleased Jean Paul's young friends.

While he was working on *The Comet,* Jean Paul asked his friend Emanuel to lend him a copy of *Don Quixote,* most probably Tieck's translation, which was finished in 1801. He kept the book for two years, but he did not like to have *The Comet* called the German *Don Quixote.*[5] Although there are points of analogy, the two books are basically different. In both novels, the comic aspect is concentrated in one symbolic figure who suffers from having a wrong perception of himself and from an abundance of imagination.[6] But reality, which both have to face, is cruel and inexorable to Don Quixote and finally unmasks his delusion.[7] Nikolaus Marggraf, on the other hand, is protected by his sister and by his friend Worble, a great bon vivant. He lives in a fantasy world, and everything turns out for the best.

Don Quixote is a tragic figure, whereas Nikolaus Marggraf is comic; for his imaginary world and reality clash only in a humorous way. He is born in Rome, not the center of the Roman world, but a very small town in Germany by that name. The old pharmacist is considered his father, but he is not, his father being some prince who remains to be found. He has a doctorate, but without having ever passed an examination; having exchanged passports with Worble, he received his friend's degree. In a financial crisis, he tries to make diamonds in a furnace. He succeeds, but perhaps only because his mother had hidden her precious stones, the prince's gift, in that same furnace. Jean Paul does not clarify this point and leaves it to the reader to combine the facts. Nikolaus cannot prove that he is a prince, but his retinue addresses him as "Your Highness." He loves the sound of the French horn and hires a horn player, who is not a horn player at all but a chimney sweep too fat to continue his profession, who does not even blow a horn but only imitates the sound of one by blowing through his lips. Nor is Nikolaus's army an army but some poor invalids who ride on both sides of his carriage.

Nikolaus has his own Raphael, who does not paint except in his dreams. Whenever he sees a great painting, he calls it a miserable copy of his own unpainted masterpiece and complains that some rascal has tried to deprive him of his fame. Nikolaus buys a prefabricated, transportable city made of wood, which he calls Nikolopolis. From this residence, which, of course, is not a city at all, he writes letters to the princess whose name and address he does not know but hopes to get in Lucastown, where a court resides. He arrives just at the birth of a real prince. The fog is impenetrable, but through the fog Nikolaus hears the shots of small mortars saluting the birth of the prince, and the excited voices of the people who are celebrating the happy event. Nobody notices him, but he is convinced that all the ovations are meant for him and enjoys his triumphant entry into the town.

Nikolaus wants to be a saint and often believes that he is one because a halo appears around his head when he is excited. There is no evil in him. In fact, he tries so hard to be good that he is moving in his naïveté and innocence.[8] He is similar to Gustav, Victor, Albano, and Walt—but as their caricature, distorted and presented ironically, and no longer as a human being. In his earlier works, Jean Paul, the poet, believed that the world could be transformed by love, friendship, sacrifice, and noble feelings. Jean Paul, the humorist, however, knew that mankind cannot be changed. He therefore allows Marggraf to escape into a world of his own, created by his imagination. In a way, Nikolaus Marggraf is a satirical portrait of Jean Paul himself which exaggerates his intense desire for knowledge and for friendship and his conceit.[9] In *Kandidat* Richter he created his youthful, idealistic image. He depicts himself as a skinny young man, running around with long hair and open shirt, who is hired by Nikolaus as a weather prophet. He is kind and protects Nikolaus, in whom he recognizes similarities with his own poetic qualities.

Nikolaus acquires a certain measure of reality through the company of his servant and laboratory assistant, Stoesser Stoss, the "pestler pestle." Like Sancho Panza, he is loyal to his master, stupid, cunning, superstitious, and always aware of his advantage. The French curses with which he decorates his speeches are as irresistibly funny as Sancho's proverbs. Jean Paul's evil genius, the "yeast of the work," [10] is the Leather Man, who calls himself Cain and is the antithesis of Nikolaus's naïve confusion. His forerunners are Matthieu in *Hesperus* and Roquairol in *Titan*. He hates mankind and serves the devil. A red snake— Cain's sign—marks his forehead. The Leather Man is looking forward to going to hell because there he will meet the souls of the indomitable animals who function by instinct and have higher knowledge than men, because man is only an imperfect ape. Through thinking, the Leather Man has transformed himself into a murderer, arsonist, poisoner, and atheist. To Jean Paul, thinking is a destructive force, isolating man and preventing him from partaking in human relationships. The thinker thus usurps the independence of the Creator.[11] In a moment of peace, which Worble procures for him by hypnotizing him, he climbs into the chimney and there, hidden by darkness, confesses with his calmest voice how much he loves all men while stating that he is condemned to hate them and serve the Prince of the World for his sins of loneliness and isolation. He suffers from a wrong image of the world, whereas Nikolaus has a wrong image of himself. Eventually, the curing of one patient would have brought about the curing of the other, but the novel stops long before it can reach a resolution.

According to Jean Paul's notes, Nikolaus was to proceed from Lucastown, where he is ignored by the court, to the City of Poets, Weimar. From there, he was to go to the City of Scholars, the City of Soldiers, the City of Lust, the City of Bigotry, and finally to the "Rollwenzelei," Mrs. Rollwenzel's inn near Bayreuth where Jean Paul used to spend part of the day writing. Nikolaus finds his princess but no throne. In the end, all the fools are cured and saved.[12] Nikolaus's life story was so much the story of Jean Paul that the latter wanted to combine the "Fiction of Nikolaus Marggraf's Life" with the "Truth of My [Jean Paul's] Life," an allusion to Goethe's autobiography, *Dichtung und Wahrheit* (*Fiction and Truth*). All the digressions were to be collected and published separately as a periodical called "Paper Kite." He gave up this plan when the writing of his biography became an unbearable burden for him. But the digressions were separated from the novel, not as a periodical but as "Enclaves" within the book. The last of these contained a list of his books, the number of works being equal to the number of his years.

CHAPTER 8

Levana; *or* The Doctrine of Education

I Prologues to the First and to the Second Editions

LEVANA was the goddess invoked by the Roman mother as she laid her newborn child at the feet of his father, who then acknowledged the infant as his own by lifting him up. *Levana* is Jean Paul's most popular work, as shown by the number of editions, interpretations, and quotations. Even Goethe, who was originally repelled by Jean Paul's style, admired *Levana* for its "incredible maturity . . . , clear presentation, wealth of comparisons and allusions." [1] Written in 1805 and 1806, the work was published in 1807 in such a hurry that it was full of typographical errors. These *errata* were published separately as *Supplement to Levana*. As early as in 1808, and again in 1811, a *Dictionary to Jean Paul's Levana* was compiled. [2]

Jean Paul's pedagogical ideas are based on his own experience as father and educator. In fact, the modern reader will note that he and Dr. Spock hold many attitudes in common. His children were one, two, and three years old when he began to write the book. Perhaps this is why the early period of childhood, "the budding," is discussed more elaborately in the first volume than "the blossoming" [3] in the second and third parts, which, in the first edition, were combined in one volume. According to Jean Paul, all important decisions are taken during the *triennium*, the first three years, when the child is still in the process of learning his language and standing on the borderline between the monkey and the man. The child is innately innocent until the parents become his "serpents on the tree" (p. 75). Here Jean Paul stands clearly under the influence of Rousseau, whose *Émile* inspired him most profoundly. No earlier work on education is comparable to it; and Jean Paul regarded all later ones as imitative of it. According to him, Basedow was Rousseau's "intelligent translator and publisher in Germany. . . . Pestalozzi is now confirming Rousseau among the people" (p. 72). In spite of the Napoleonic wars, the first edition of *Levana* was out of print in 1811, which means that, in spite of the "warlike Vesuvius and Etna" (p. 77), German parents took time to inform themselves on how to improve their children's education.

II *Importance and Principles of Education*

For Jean Paul education meant moral development; he invariably refers to intellectual development as instruction. There is no question about the importance of educating the young, but, Jean Paul asks, can it be done? In order to show the difficulties and prove the possibility, he invents the inaugural discourse of a young teacher who introduces himself to the faculty by proving that education has no effect on students. He is immediately dismissed, but given the opportunity to lecture a second and last time and impress upon his audience the importance of "The Educational Chair." With these two speeches, Jean Paul gives his serious topic a humorous form.

After two prologues and two contradictory speeches, the author goes *in medias res*, introducing the reader to the "Spirit and Principle of Education." First of all, the educator must know his goal. But, normally, fathers have a diversity of goals, and mothers give a hundred orders at a time, followed by counter-orders. Another danger for children are the educators who are concerned only "for appearance and political usefulness" (p. 108). The Spartans who killed their infants when they were physically handicapped were hardly more cruel than modern parents, who educate their children to be bankers and lawyers, rather than happy, moral people.

The child needs a certain freedom for his development, because he has within himself "an ideal man" (p. 111) whom he tries to liberate and of whom he is most strongly aware in his youth.[4] Education, then, is simply the assistance of the teacher in liberating the ideal man. This can only be achieved, however, if the teacher is capable of recognizing this man. But how can the ideal man be defined? "It is that in others on which our reliance, friendship, or enmity rests. . . . It is that which unites all esthetic, moral, and intellectual powers in one soul. If one must translate the perfect and ideal man into words, one might perhaps say that it is the harmonious maximum of all the individual qualities taken together" (p. 116). When Jean Paul was asked how a teacher could recognize the character of his student, he replied that he would have to write not one book but books about it. Even more than books the teacher needs a talent to find the hidden undeveloped character of the child. "But alas! three things are very difficult to discover and to impart: to have a character—to describe one—to find one" (p. 116).[5]

Jean Paul begins his investigation with the moment of conception. He regrets the carelessness and irresponsibility of parents and governments who do not even try to learn more about the possibilities of protecting, regulating, and influencing the physical and spiritual formation of the child. He then rejects all nursery tales about the influence of the mother on the foetus during pregnancy. When the child is born, "at last the child can say to the father—Educate me, for I breathe" (p. 142). All first impressions—for instance, the first music, the first color—are strongest; therefore children must not be exposed to overly violent or sweet experiences.

During the first three years, the "speechless period" (p. 143), children need, most of all, warmth and cheerfulness. A small child suffers more intensely than a mature person because he cannot escape into hope or reason. Dreams and illness cause fear and terror in children; therefore parents should stave off additional fears as long as the child is young. Cheerfulness and joy are salutary but must not be confused with pleasure, for, while animals experience pleasure, only human beings can be serene. Children should not be prematurely driven out of their Paradise, which is lost by pleasure. Cheerfulness comes from play and activity. A toy gives pleasure by its appearance and joy by its use. But this joy must not be too intense. "In one month of twenty-nine days a child might be mentally destroyed if one could make out of every day a first Christmas Day" (p. 148). Only activity gives genuine cheerfulness; and activity, for a child, means playing.

For the child, toys are alive; a doll is a living being because there is no understanding of death. The child thinks objects are animate and says, for instance, "The lights have covered themselves up, they have gone to bed—the spring has dressed itself—the water creeps down the glass—his house lives there—the wind dances—or, speaking of a watch whose works are removed, 'It is not alive'" (p. 154). And toys that are too elaborate kill the imagination. Thus Jean Paul noted that his daughter Emma preferred a bootjack or her old wooden Cinderella doll to an elegant, overdressed doll prima donna. Furthermore, toys and picture books have to be taken away as soon as the imagination is tired of them. A good picture book does not show isolated objects but combines them in actions familiar to the child. Pictures and toys should be small, like the child, who otherwise would always be surrounded by giants. The best toy, even for children weary of play, is sand, which can be used for building and throwing, as water, seeds, or flour, and as a foundation for writing and painting.

Jean Paul felt that the best playmates for children were children, for only they are childish enough for each other, as their imaginations complement each other. To meet other children on the playground is the first encounter with society; and to give a good hiding to another boy, or to take one, is more effective than a father's or a teacher's punishment. The best play for children is conversation among themselves or with parents, who should be eloquent when they are happy and reserved when they are angry. Play and rest must be well proportioned, even against the will of the child, who demands a continous, accelerating progression of pleasures. Because of the child's excitability there should be a few toys, neatly arranged at night; a period of relaxation and boredom before bedtime; and no company after awakening (certainly not that of parents).

Jean Paul devotes a whole chapter of *Levana* to the dancing of children. He does not recommend ballet lessons, modern dance, or any drill, but only their jumping and whirling around, in couples, in rows, in circles, accompanied by music. Dancing should take up several hours a day because it is the best training of all muscles, giving equal exercise to all of them, whereas sport trains and hardens specific muscles. In addition to dancing, children must sing, father and mother singing for, and with, them. Singing is a better exercise than screaming, which doctors praise so highly for the invigoration of the lungs. On the whole, music is a more cheerful skill than poetry. Men can happily fall asleep listening to imaginary music, and a child is best awakened by music. Montaigne's father did so because he was afraid that a sudden sharp noise might damage the brain of his sleeping son.

In spite of his admiration for Rousseau, Jean Paul wrote two chapters against Rousseau's theories on "Commands, Prohibitions, Punishments, and Crying." He felt that Rousseau's method was good for mature people who understand the law of necessity which reason teaches them to respect. A child needs his parents' words to guide him rather than the physical consequences of his misdeeds to teach him. Here he preferred to follow Basedow's suggestions.[6] He apologizes for not offering theories or a system but simply presenting a collection of experiences. In the first place, he asks parents not to emphasize prohibition but rather the free action of the child. If they have to forbid something, they should do it with words, not with abrupt action. They must not snatch away a knife that the child holds in his hand but have the child put it down after having heard the parent's explanation of why he must not have it, thus acting on his own and not obeying a prohibition.

Parents who want their child's obedience based on love, gratitude, and voluntary resignation rather than submission must be capable of the same motivations for their own actions. In that case, they may ask the child gently to do them a favor. If this favor is granted, they must thank the child, showing their pleasure. If the favor is refused, they must not punish the child: "Even the camel moves no more swiftly before the whip, only behind the flute." Jean Paul actually hesitates to use of word "punishment" and prefers to speak of pain or "afterburn." Only a person who feels guilty can be punished, but young children, like animals, have no guilt feelings. The basic error of parents is that they consider their children's shortcomings to be worse than their own. And when the child differs from them they call him wrong. Jean Paul was the advocate of ill-treated children whom he defended against their torturers, parents and teachers alike. He was, of course, opposed to corporal punishment, with the exception of the rod, which he wished to be used occasionally as "paradigm and threat for the future; afterwards the mere threatening preaches and restrains" (p. 175). But a child who hits another person must be hit immediately, preferably by the attacked person himself. If the child is hit by another child, a girl may ask her father for protection, but a boy must always hit back right away, or he will never grow up to be a man.

Children are inclined to lie, and if they are successful, they will feel encouraged to tell more lies. "Tremblingly" (p. 175)

Jean Paul advises the educator to ask suggestive questions in order to prevent the child from lying. For instance, when the educator is almost sure that the child played, against his order, on a frozen lake, he should ask: "Who was with you?" or: "How long were you there?" Then the child will be so confused by the apparent omniscience of the interrogator that the bold lie, "I was not on the lake," will be cut short.

More important than the punishment is its aftermath, i.e., the transition to forgiveness. "After the hour of storm every seed-word finds a softened warm ground" (p. 176). When the mother explains with a low voice how much she suffers from the misdeed, the child's pain will be soothed, too. But women are inclined to postpone the moment of forgiveness; they like to pout and bear the guilty child—or husband—a grudge. Children who, like animals, live in the present time and are able to enjoy life right after the punishment, might learn to get along without their mother's love and pardon, or they might become embittered.

The educator is not allowed to tell a child: "You are a liar," or, "You are bad." He can only say, "You told a lie," or, "This is a bad deed." The action can be condemned, but not the person. The child must never feel dishonored. "Shame is the cold Orcus of the inner man, a spiritual hell, without redemption, wherein the damned can become nothing else but at most one devil more" (p. 178).

The end of the first volume of *Levana* gains emphasis from Jean Paul's far-reaching words on the trustfulness of children. He preaches not like a theologian but like a child's friend. When the child sees in his parents infallible beings, when he believes in them without proof, when he asks confidently for their help in spiritual need, he receives from them the immeasurable treasure of faith in another being. Adults willingly believe in learned people, such as specialists, in certain fields. They are eager to know the opinions of great men who seem to know more about the nature of our being. But there is a difference between believing in a person and having faith in him. Lovers and friends have faith in each other, and a religious person has faith in god, and "this is the Peter's rock, the fast foundation of human worth" (p. 185), which Jean Paul wants children to be given: "He who rightly trusts shows that he has seen the deity face to face; and there is, perhaps, no higher moral gratification on earth than this—if sense and testimony attack your friend in your heart to hurl him thence, even then to stand by him with the God in you, to preserve and love him, not as formerly, but more deeply" (p. 186). It is interesting to note that no European pedagogue before Jean Paul mentioned the necessity of trustfulness and love as the foundation of education. It cannot even be found in Rousseau's *Émile*, which is considered to constitute the beginning of modern psychology.

III *Female Education*

The "Appendix to the Third Fragment," at the beginning of the second volume, is, for the modern reader, the most humorous chapter of the whole work. The subtitle "On Physical Education" is misleading; for it is really a chapter on hygiene written in the form of a letter to his young friend Paul Emil Thieriot, who had no children and was not even engaged to be married when Jean Paul wrote this chapter. In this fictitious letter to a newlywed three months before the delivery of the first child, Jean Paul gives, for the most part, seemingly self-evident suggestions, which must, nonetheless, have been unacceptable to mothers of his time, or at least to his own wife Karoline. His remark that the birth of the first child is the end of the honeymoon, that Thieriot's fictitious wife, having been pregnant for six months only, is still obedient, which will no longer be the case after the delivery—these and other ironical hints at the stubbornness of wives reflect Jean Paul's own reactions to Karoline's pedagogical bias. He showed his triumph over Karoline when he added the following sentence to the first paragraph of the second edition: "Some readers will not agree so theoretically with this letter as my children, who during the printing and distribution of the first edition were educated in accordance with it, did practically, by their flourishing condition" (p. 188).

The "Comic Appendix and Epilogue to the First Volume, a 'Dreamed' Letter to the late Professor Gellert in which the Author Begs for a Tutor" is announced as a relaxation and diversion for reader and author. It is really a satire on private teachers in the form of a letter. Here Jean Paul asks Christian Fürchtegott Gellert, who was famous for helping other people with their private difficulties, for a teacher, for he himself has no time to educate his son Max because he is writing a book on education! It is hard to find a good teacher; even Gellert himself would not be the ideal teacher, although his naïve friendliness and ease are laudable. But Jean Paul is looking for "a very hard material—mind" (p. 206). He blames teachers for giving too many orders and for writing the Ten Commandments on the door of the pupil's room, the surest way to have the child overlook them. Incessant teaching while the child is awake, even during a walk, produces a listening slave and cripples the child.

Jean Paul anticipates Gellert's answer by referring to a humorous French anecdote of a young preacher who had forgotten his sermon and did not know what to say: "However, he composed himself, raised his voice . . . and proclaimed to his audience, with rare energy, one conjunction after another—*enfin, car, donc, si, or*—and muttered with falling voice all kind of matter between the particles . . ." (p. 209). The congregation thought they had the wrong seats, either too close or too far from the pulpit, and when their "soul-curer" pronounced the "Amen," they acclaimed him as a true orator. And what do children remember of their teacher's preaching other than some thousand ifs, becauses, therefores? Don't they stop listening as soon as the teacher begins to admonish them?

Jean Paul also ridicules the overload of teaching material by asking the envisioned educator to teach his son not a thousand languages but only—seven. In addition to eight daily lessons, dancing, swimming, riding, fencing, singing, and playing the violin, the piano and wind instruments must be covered, too. The Sundays and the holidays must be used for "the inculcation of many virtues" (p. 214). In the middle of this humorous satire, Jean Paul becomes suddenly serious when he says of the future educator of his son: "He will—since liberality is in any case inestimable, and why not then primarily in education—treat him with practical freedom and power, and not deprive him of his own rights. He will find little fault with what is childish . . . will draw him on to what is great and universal . . . will be rather the physician to his weakness than the extinguisher of his strength" (p. 210).

The fourth fragment on education for women contains the most popular quotations on the role of the mother; they deserve their fame for their substance and form. Jean Paul addresses mothers in the tone of the paean: "It is true that the sacrifices you make for the world will be little known by it—men govern and earn the glory; and the thousand watchful nights and sacrifices by which a mother purchases a hero or a poet for the state are forgotten, not once counted; for the mothers themselves do not count them; and so, one century after another, unnamed and unthanked, send forth the arrows, the suns, the storm-birds, and the nightingales of time!" (p. 226). The only reward a mother receives is to be remembered by her child.

This hymn to mothers is contrasted with a satire in the form of a confession. "Madame Jacqueline," the counterpart of Jean Jacques Rousseau, choosing Jean Paul as her father-confessor, provides him with a long list of her pedagogical sins. She confesses, for instance, that she never stuck to her orders for more than a month. She often forbade something, only half conscious of what she was saying and without watching whether she was obeyed or not. In moments of great happiness, she was unable to deny a favor. In the presence of guests, she allowed herself "pedagogical vacations," respecting her guest more than her five children. Last year, for instance, some needlework, the visit of her best friend, an interesting novel had prevented her from seeing her two younger children other than at breakfast. But in other years she had embraced and educated them fervently, twice a day for a couple of hours. She feels that she has expected too much response from them, which made her son angry and her daughter hypocritical. She has listened to her husband's advice without following it. "Did not mine positively, seriously desire, that when I occasionally washed the little thing, I would not rub his face and wipe it sharply up and down; 'because,' said he, 'this kind of violence is disagreeable to them and excites their passion'; but that I would softly rub downwards and then gently round? What ridiculous pedantry! Surely a woman must know how to wash! So I go on just as usual, and care not how loudly both little and big cry out against it" (p. 220).

But not all mothers are pedagogical sinners like Madame Jacqueline. Jean Paul is fair to middle-class women who, during the first five years, are with their children day and night. To him, this physical strain explains a mother's emotional instability. It is easy for the father to be clearheaded and logical, since he sees the child only for a short time. He can help his wife by appreciating her work and by being her constant lover. Like Pestalozzi, Jean Paul assigns the responsibility for the education of the small child to the mother. He was thoroughly familiar with Pestalozzi's *Wie Gertrud ihre Kinder lehrt* and his *Buch der Mütter*.[7]

Before presenting "The Education of Girls" in twelve paragraphs, Jean Paul devotes eight paragraphs to "The Nature of Girls." He sees a great similarity between women and children, as contrasted with men. "The same unbroken unity of nature—the same clear perception and understanding of the present—the same sharpness of wit—the keen spirit of observation—ardour and quietness—excitability and easily raised emotions—the ready quick passage from the inward to the outward, and conversely, from gods to ribbons, from motes in the sunbeam to solar systems . . . " (p. 228).

The worth of these general statements may be debatable; but when Jean Paul discusses the education of girls, it becomes evident how much the emancipation that has taken place during the last century and a half has changed our judgment of women. Thus modern education has changed decisively the young girl's attitude towards men. Jean Paul describes the feeling of a "fresh virgin heart" that experiences the first unsurpassable love for a God-Man who, "for a being hitherto bound to a little corner of the world, suddenly reveals a whole new world which is, for the maiden, this world joined with the next. Who then shall restrain the gratitude of love towards him who has opened happiness and freedom to a mind chained to the narrow present, who has embodied all those dreams which formerly the unoccupied soul personified in the stars, in spring-time, in friends, in childlike duties?" (p. 236). While modern women may smile at Jean Paul's dream of the adoring bride, they will violently disagree when, right after the honeymoon, he describes them as "withered on the marital pitchfork," [8] a comparison to which even the editor of the first edition objected.

Jean Paul sees the purpose of women in motherhood. For this end, nature has equipped them with physical attraction and a unique capability to love. After the first child is born, the love for the husband is replaced by the mother's love for the child. With this assumption in mind, the education of girls seems to mean nothing but training them as mothers, i.e., educators. But Jean Paul's conclusion is different; he wants to create a harmonious human being. Therefore, a girl's potential motherhood must be the guiding hand of her education, not its end.

Another "Commandment of Female Education," the "gymnastics of life and labor" (p. 250), is the abolishment of needlework and, with it, the physical disadvantage of a sedentary life. Girls must be given work that requires new ideas and concentration. A *dolce far niente* produces forgetfulness, absentmindedness and lack of presence of mind, which is a weakness. The twentieth century has done away with ladies whose only voluntary physical exercise is dancing. The dangers of sedentary work, however, are still known to us, albeit nowadays they are caused by sedentary professions. It is evident that Jean Paul would be surprised to see modern women not only responsible for their household but providing for it, and to learn that, in professional life, they have equal duties with men, in addition to being mothers and wives. But his nice, old-fashioned object is still a perfectly good one: to bring up girls in such a way that they can make their children and husbands happy.

Jean Paul will not fight against female vanity. No man can realize the triumph of a beautiful woman "who carrying her nose, her eyes, her figure, her complexion, as sparkling jewels through the streets, blinds one eye after another with her dazzling brilliance, and risks no capital in exchange for her profits" (p. 260).

A whole paragraph of *Levana* is devoted to the cheerfulness of girls, forbidding grumbling mothers to prevent their children from laughing. The mothers, who have "passed out of the triumphant church of virgins into the church militant of matrons" (p. 265), cannot sympathize with the merriment of their daughters. They must never curtail a young girl's irresistible urge to laugh. Life is serious; therefore young people must be given the freedom to enjoy the short moment of joy before the trials of mature age begin. Jean Paul raves about the beauty and charm of a young girl who laughs and has a sense of fun, but still shows no signs of irony or satire. He would marry the girl who laughs at his jokes, as is the custom "among a certain Lybian people" (p. 265).

Jean Paul concludes the second volume with maxims for educators, which he writes down in advance in case a visitor should ask him for a few "useful impromptu thoughts" (p. 306). Only two of these maxims need be quoted here, although all of them could serve as polestars to teachers. "Tutor! Have at heart no work of your pupil so much as love of work; it is the latter he should learn by the former.—What more excellent object can a teacher set before himself than to accustom his pupil never to say an important yes or no, never to express a like or dislike, without taking an hour's respite to consider the question, request, or sin? With such a period of grace he might write himself a brevet of infallibility" (p. 307).

IV *Male Education*

While the first volume of *Levana* began with two introductions and a pair of opposed speeches, and the second one with one appendix and a comical appendix to the first volume, the third one devotes itself to the education of boys, beginning with their moral education. According to Jean Paul, the development of moral strength begins with the cultivation of physical strength. Boys must be wild and aggressive; their fights with other boys, climbing trees and falling, being obstinate and headstrong are their best preparation for life. "Out of the wild English youth there grows a thoughful member of Parliament as out of the early Roman robbers a virtuous self-sacrificing senate arose" (p. 313).

The second stage of the education towards moral strength and courage is the endurance of pain. Jean Paul forbids parents to show any pity for their boys' pains. Nor must parents show any fear in the presence of their children because the correct response to fear is the third stage towards moral strength. Similarly, parents can help a child overcome his fear of dreams by analyzing them—"These gigantic chaotic painters in the mind shape out of the little terrors of the day those monstrous masks of the Furies which form and nourish that fear of ghosts which slumbers in every human being" (p. 317). He distinguishes between fear which instead of courage can be man's reaction to the future and the creatures of his imagination, and terror which supplants courage in the face of the evils of the present. Courage is not blindness in the face of danger, but rather the resolve to overcome dangers by recognizing them. Terror can be felt only once; but a basic fear that is deeply rooted in every child can be mitigated by the parents' cheerful calm.

"One ruling idea in the heart" (p. 321), such as the search for knowledge or the love for his country, will strengthen the boy's moral power. A weakling is capable of a single noble deed when he is carried away by a momentary emotion. But real greatness presupposes a steady inner fire that lasts the entire life. Nobody can teach such "steadfast will," but Jean Paul believes that everybody has an innate ideal that can be awakened, by reading Plutarch, for instance, or by hearing of the sacrifices displayed in wars of freedom. Some educators will criticize him for overstressing the necessity of giving young people ideals, which are the stuff of fiction, not of reality. But young people need ideals to guide them. Later they will incorporate their ideals into reality: "The ripe sunflower no longer turns its heavy seed-laden head toward the sun" (p. 328).

The second chapter is entirely devoted to truthfulness, which means for Jean Paul "the act of telling the truth intentionally, even to the injury of oneself" (p. 329). Weaklings tell lies even when they would rather not; any threat drives them to dishonesty. Jean Paul describes the lie as that "devouring cancer of the inner man" (p. 329) which makes him more infamous in the eyes of the people than in the eyes of philosophers. Men avoid false words, asserts Jean Paul, more assiduously than false deeds; and a word seems to weigh more heavily on the conscience than action. Jean Paul's explanation of this fact shows his deep respect for speech as reason incarnate and as the instrument of the poet. "Two individuals stand in relation to each other as upon separate islands, locked up within the prison bars of bones and behind the curtain of skin. Mere motion shows me only life, but not its reasons. The animated eye of a Raphael Madonna often speaks to us from the canvas, which yet houses no mind; wax figures are hollow; and the ape, our mocking image, is dumb. In what glorified form, then, does the human soul reveal itself? In speech only, in reason thus made man, in this audible freedom" (p. 331). By telling a lie, people destroy all contact between themselves; only bodies remain visible, while the inner life is destroyed.

During the first five years of their lives, children tell neither lies nor the truth; they simply talk. Speaking is such a wonderful experience for them that they often talk nonsense, just in order to enjoy their new ability. Sometimes they think aloud, saying yes and no concurrently. Sometimes they do not know a word we use in asking a question, therefore their answer is not false but erroneous. And sometimes they report their dreams which are as true for them as reality. There are only two real lies that children tell; when they try to get something with a lie or when they are afraid to admit a misdeed. What can be done in such a case? Either the parent must appear omniscient, or, better still, he remains in the dark, because questioning the child is too painful. If, however, a lie is proven, the parent must express abhorrence and even punish, the best punishment being to impose silence on the child who so abused the gift of speech.

Physical strength and truthfulness are the first two stages of the good education, the third being the "Education of the Affections" (p. 338). Jean Paul does not define love or affection; and the book he planned to write on this subject was never written.[9] Within the context of his *Levana*, he only refutes selfish women who confuse love with infatuation. He also defies philosophers who, with the exception of Plato, Hemsterhuis, Fritz Jacobi, and Herder, have defined love as an instinct "utterly below their categorical imperative" or as a "kind of rational regard ["Vernunftliebe"]" (p. 338). Love is an innate faculty that must either be developed or tempered according to the share of love that has fallen to a child. The infant is selfish like an animal, his only concern being to satify his needs. His innate love, however, will first break through in a feeling of pity. The educator cannot create this feeling; he can only remove the "moss and briars of selfishness" (p. 340) that keep it from growing.

The best way to awaken love is to try to put oneself into somebody else's position and to develop a respect for life in general. This precept takes literary form in *Siebenkäs*, where Leibgeber and Siebenkäs symbolically exchange their names and Leibgeber subsequently gives up his whole existence so that his friend can take his identity after his presumed death. A child is first taught a deep respect for the life of animals. Like cattle-loving Brahmins or like primitive people who recognize "in everything the universal life of the Godhead" (p. 343), the child must feel close to all animals and plants and never kill voluntarily. If parents "admit all living things into the human family" (p. 346), the child will develop a feeling for them that is more encompassing than pity.

In order to teach a higher love than that of Ovid's *Ars Amatoria*, parents can awaken benevolence by describing not other people's needs but the future happiness that will ensue from the child's help. The happy approval and praise of the parents will encourage the child to give increasingly more help to others. Another "love-potion" (p. 347) is love for love. Affectionate words and looks reveal love to a child more easily than deeds, because a child is still innocent enough to take his parents' acts of sacrifice for granted. Kissing and embracing are often a burden for a child whose "buds are still closed" (p. 347). Gifts are an indirect way of expressing love, whereas words and looks express our feelings directly. The Ten Commandments will become superfluous when the child is taught how to love. "Teach them to love, I repeat; that means—*do you love!*" (p. 350).

Jean Paul saw the great advantage of his "pamphlet" (!) in its slimness (although *Levana* has more than 350 pages). He felt he could afford to write a "Supplementary Appendix to Moral Education" without tiring the reader. One interesting paragraph of this appendix deals with children's books. The best story they can be told is that of the parents' own childhood experience. Children love small things. To see their giant parents portrayed as small as they are attaches them more closely to them. To hear that they, too, had to obey, that they, too, were punished, and that they loved their parents impresses them favorably. Next to their own autobiography, parents should prefer Oriental stories, *The Arabian Nights,* for instance, because parents should avoid all stories that teach a moral. Stories of great dangers and most marvelous rescues, or stories full of humor will make children happy. Jean Paul even suggests taking children to the opera, to *The Magic Flute* for instance, in order to imbue them with the romantic world of magic and fairies.

The last paragraph of the Appendix gives advice to parents and teachers on how to handle "sensual faults" (p. 361). Prudishness and the hint, "This is only for adults, you will find out later," are the wrong answers when the child asks for sexual information. An exact answer does not hurt a child because he understands less than we think and is satisfied, like many adults, with the penultimate cause, without asking for the ultimate. If the child is older, an analytical lecture starting, for instance, with the heart, will bring the child to boredom and thus to satisfaction. In spite of all desirable frankness, the child should be spared the description of the act of begetting because of the "external similarity of action between men and beasts" (p. 365). During the critical years, when the child is twelve to fifteen years old and full of revolution and evolution, fascinating projects that keep his mind busy will be helpful. The best means to avoid sexual problems is coeducation, "for two boys will keep twelve girls, or two girls twelve boys, innocent amidst winks, jokes and improprieties . . . merely by that instinctive sense which is the forerunner of matured modesty. But I will guarantee nothing in a school where girls are alone together, and still less where boys are" (p. 362).

In the fragment "On the Development of the Desire for Intellectual Progress," the reader is not surprised to learn that Jean Paul turns away from the pre-Pestalozzian method of piling up facts or squeezing as many data as possible into the pupil's brains, since the title of this fragment contains a program in itself. Surface knowledge produces "heirs of all ideas, but originators none" (p. 366). Only the desire to know must be strengthened, since this desire differentiates men from beasts. "The developments of this formative power are first, language, and secondly, observation; both of which by defining and stressing an idea bring it more accurately before the mind; thirdly, imagination, which can retain an entire series of ideas, thus rendering from it the relationship unknown but sought for and thus anticipated, either as part, consequence, foundation, symbol, or image; fourthly, wit; fifthly, reflection; sixthly, memory" (p. 367).

To the first point of his six-point program Jean Paul adds that a thorough knowledge of the mother tongue is more important than being fluent in foreign languages. The child's way of conquering the surrounding world of appearances is to give the correct names to the things in it. Although during the first ten years all objects must be carefully analyzed, no spiritual problems should be scrutinized because innate ideas might be destroyed by premature discussion. But so far as objects are concerned, the child must be required to search for the correct expression and never be satisfied with a vague word derived from a vague mental image. A child should be exposed to long sentences, even to puns and contradictory statements, such as "I heard this with my eyes," or "This is beautiful-ugly." Such exercises force the child to think. Even when he does not understand individual words, the accent and the intonation will help him to grasp the meaning of the whole, thus training his power of synthesis. Adults should never use baby talk, but rather a vocabulary that is a few years ahead of the child's language because "the child already carries half his world, that of mind—the objects, for instance, of moral and metaphysical contemplation—ready formed within him; hence . . . language, being provided only with physical images, cannot form but merely illustrate his mental conceptions" (pp. 370-71). Pestalozzi's formal education and Jean Paul's method seem to be similar in this respect. Both educators stress the necessity of clear perception and the precise appellation of the object. For Jean Paul, however, this is only one step in the child's education leading to his intellectual maturity, whereas Pestalozzi sees in it the only way to knowledge of reality.[10]

The desire for intellectual progress is further developed by "Attention and the Power of Adaptive Combination" ("Vorbildungskraft"). In this chapter, Jean Paul distinguishes between the power of attention "diffused among the generality of men" and that "belonging solely to men of genius" (p. 377). The intense, intuitive attention of the genius must be respected and cherished by the teacher. But the average students, like adults, have difficulty maintaining interest and must be taught how to concentrate. Uninterrupted attention is impossible for human beings; therefore Jesuits, for instance, were not allowed to study for more than two hours at a time. Jean Paul suggests three rules to help a child concentrate on a single object: ask him questions; follow Pestalozzi's method of analyzing the object; or develop the child's "power of intellectual synthesis" (p. 378).

Mathematics trains the child to deal with long combinations of numbers, algebraic relationships, and sets of geometric ideas, exercises which strengthen his power for intellectual synthesis. *Vorbildungskraft*, as Jean Paul calls it, is neither imagination nor memory, but rather the capacity to survey and "fit together chains of ideas,"[11] a capacity essential to the philosopher in his reasoning, to the mathematician in his calculations, and equally so, to the inventor in his fabrications "by retaining in connection and presenting in order the daily increasing masses of ideas, numbers, lines and images" (p. 381). All flexibility of ideas is based on these long chains formed with the help of the power of adaptive combination. Children must be trained to build bridges from one subject to the other, to have intellectual flexibility, i.e., to combine, compare, and handle concurrently ideas with ease. But in the German school, Jean Paul stated, they are supposed to have their thoughts "as immovably fixed as their buttocks" (p. 383). If children are encouraged to develop their intellect, they will gain perfect ease in combining ideas, and by this they will finally become the masters of ideas. The examples from Jean Paul's "Anthology of My Pupils' Bons Mots," quoted on page 21f. of this book, show that he was fully capable of focusing his students' knowledge, so that their puns and witty formulations were good enough to print.

According to Jean Paul, the teacher must also focus his attention on the development of his student's recollection, a function not identical with memory. Memory is a *receptive* faculty, depending largely on physical conditions, but recollection is a *productive* faculty which discovers a relationship between ideas retained by the memory. Pythagoras asked his students to recall every day's events before falling asleep in order to strengthen their recollection. A teacher should ask his students to summarize stories or fairy tales for the same purpose, or to learn by heart an entire chapter of a favorite book in a foreign language, instead of memorizing the unconnected words of a vocabulary. Thorough mastery of a subject is only attained by concentrating for a long time. Therefore Jean Paul would rather teach one subject for a whole month than change the subjects five times a day: "What a probability of growth in twelve branches during the year" (p. 391).

The last fragment of *Levana*, "Ninth Fragment or Keystone," contains six short paragraphs and one longer paragraph in which Jean Paul accounts for the purpose of his work, which, he explains, offers neither a theory of instruction nor a theory of remedies. Unlike Rousseau, he does not send a single little "sun-god" to school alone, because he is certain that education can only be effective with groups of children. The emphasis in the first five years of the educative process must be on physical developments, the intellect being thus left free for later endeavors. Jean Paul attacks society and government bitterly in his catalogues of the suffering of both children and teachers. The former kind of suffering comes from barbarous punishments, like kneeling on peas or sharp pieces of wood, the latter from their penurious incomes. The last paragraph of the book is even more ominous and calls to mind the apocalyptic visions of chaos which have been threatening us since the fission of the atom. Jean Paul asks, "What, then, are children really?" (p. 412). His answer, in the form of a poem, is a somewhat sentimental vision of children as angelic beings coming to this danger-filled, sinful earth. This "Poem of the Last Day and the Last Two Children" is, of course, not the real end of *Levana*. Jean Paul simply has to add a *Supplement to Levana* with two extremely witty prologues and sixteen chapters containing the *errata* of *Levana* and of nine of his other works. But this supplement need not be discussed here.

In his dissertation on Pestalozzi and Jean Paul, Anton Luible points out that both pedagogues avoided the one-sided tendency of most Enlightenment thinkers to stress the development of reason at the expense of the emotions. A systematization of Jean Paul's ideas was successfully undertaken by Wilhelm Münch and subsequently realized in the experiments of the Waldorf Schools.[12]

Epilogue

THOMAS CARLYLE'S first essay on Jean Paul, published in 1827, introduced the poet to the English-speaking audience. About one hundred articles on Jean Paul were published in the United States between 1802 and 1880, one third of which originated in New England; the rest emanated from New York, Philadelphia, Ohio, and the South.[1] In New England, the most intense interest came between 1846 and 1862. These were the "sentimental years" of New England culture during which the people basked in material well-being and could afford to indulge an interest in the emotional outpourings of such writers as Jean Paul, in all "that is beautiful . . . and mysteriously sublime."[2] Others were attracted to Jean Paul as a moralist. The Moravian Brothers, for instance, could find their own image in the protagonist of Jean Paul's first novel, *The Invisible Lodge*. Karl Follen at Harvard University, Henry Wadsworth Longfellow at Smith College, Frederic Henry Hedge, Professor of German at Harvard and one of the founders of the Concord Transcendentalist group, all inspired their students to study this prolific and abstruse German author. His best English translator, Charles Timothy Brooks, was one of Follen's students. All of the Jean Paul scholars in America were convinced that the rewards justified the effort, whether one gained satisfaction from the pure intellectual exercise of coping with the "Colossus"[3] or simply took pleasure in the beauties of his prose. The conviction was that both esthetically and ethically Jean Paul provided enrichment for the reader. Our study—without trying to compete with these illustrious predecessors—has the same purpose: to encourage the student to read Jean Paul's work. Because, to quote the man himself, "there is really no other way to understand a great author except by reading him ten times."[4]

Notes and References

Where no source for a translation is given, the author is responsible for the text.

Preface

1. Karl Freye, as quoted by Margarete Reckling-Altenheim, *Jean Paul's Reception in the 19th and 20th Centuries. An Abridgment of Thesis*, New York University (New York, 1938), p. 13.

2. Ernst Robert Curtius, *European Literature and the Latin Middle Ages*, tr. Willard R. Trask (New York, Pantheon Books, Bollingen Series XXXVI, 1953), p. 274.

3. Goethe, *West-Östlicher Divan*, Jubiläumsausgabe (Stuttgart und Berlin, 1902-1907), V, 219.

4. Jean Paul, "Die wunderbare Gesellschaft in der Neujahrsnacht," as quoted by Joachim Bodamer, *Jean Paul als Prophet unserer Zeit* (Stuttgart, 1958), p. 28.

5. Hugo von Hofmannsthal, "Jean Paul," *Gesammelte Werke in Einzelausgaben*, Prosa III (Frankfurt, 1952), p. 154.

6. *Ibid.*

Chapter One

1. Eduard Berend, ed. and introd., *Jean Pauls Werke* (Berlin, 1923), I, iii-xxxvi. Hereafter cited as *Jean Pauls Werke*.

2. *Life of Jean Paul Friedrich Richter: Compiled from Various Sources; Together with His Autobiography*, tr. Eliza Buckminster Lee (London, 1845), p. 9. Hereafter cited as Lee.

3. Max Kommerell, *Jean Paul*, 4th ed. (Frankfurt, 1966), p. 11. Hereafter cited as Kommerell.

4. Lee, pp. 56-57.

5. *Ibid.*, p. 53.

6. *Ibid.*

7. *Ibid.*, p. 67.

8. *Jean Pauls Sämtliche Werke: Historisch-Kritische Ausgabe*, ed. Eduard Berend (Weimar, 1927 ff.; Berlin, 1952 ff.), Sec. 1, I, 58. Hereafter cited as *Werke*.

9. *Ibid.*, p. 23.

10. See Jean Paul's "Nachlass," Capsule X, Deutsche Staatsbibliothek, Berlin.

11. Lee, pp. 75-76.
12. *Wahrheit aus Jean Pauls Leben,* eds. Christian Otto (vols. I-III), Ernst Förster (vols. IV-VI), (Breslau, 1826-1833), VI, 154-55.
13. *Ibid.,* p. 161.
14. *Ibid.,* p. 162.

Chapter Two

1. *Jean Pauls Werke,* I, 2.
2. *Schillers Werke:* Nationalausgabe, eds. Lieselotte Blumenthal, Benno von Wiese (Weimar, 1962), XX, 466-67; 472.
3. *Werke,* Sec. 1, XI, 241-44.
4. *Ibid.,* II, liv.
5. Kommerell, p. 287.
6. Friedrich Hebbel's letter to Emil Kuh as quoted by Berend in *Jean Pauls Werke,* I, 3.
7. *Werke,* Sec. 1, XI, 190.
8. *Jean Pauls Werke,* I, 5.
9. *Ibid.,* p. 9.
10. *Ibid.,* p. 16.
11. *Ibid.,* p. 18.
12. Kommerell, p. 285.
13. *Werke,* Sec. 1, XIII, XCIII.
14. *Ibid.,* p. lxxxix.
15. *Ibid.,* p. 410; the following five quotations are taken from the same text.
16. *Jean Pauls Persönlichkeit in Berichten der Zeitgenossen,* 2nd, rev., ed., ed. Eduard Berend (Berlin and Weimar, 1956), p. 329.
17. *Werke,* Sec. 1, XIII, 511.
18. *Ibid.,* p. 512.
19. *Ibid.,* p. 516.

Chapter Three

1. K. Ph. Moritz as quoted by Paul Nerrlich, *Jean Paul* (Berlin, 1889), p. 211. Hereafter cited as Nerrlich.
2. *Ibid.,* p. 214.
3. See Bernhard Boeschenstein, "Jean Pauls Romankonzeption," *Deutsche Romantheorien,* ed. Reinhold Grimm, (Frankfurt, 1968), p. 126. Hereafter cited as Boeschenstein.
4. *Ibid.*

5. Eduard Berend, "Vorwort," *Werke*, Sec. 1, II, xxxvi.

6. Edward V. Brewer, "Jean Paul's *Unsichtbare Loge* and Early Romanticism," *The Germanic Review*, VIII (1933), p. 170.

7. See *Werke*, Sec. 1, II, xl.

8. *Jean Pauls Werke*, ed. by Norbert Miller, (Munich, 1960 ff.), I, 177. Hereafter cited as Miller I.

9. Jean Paul Friedrich Richter, *The Invisible Lodge*, tr. Charles T. Brooks, (New York, 1883), p. 275. Hereafter cited as *Lodge*.

10. *Ibid.*

11. *Ibid.*, p. 276.

12. *Ibid.*, p. 277.

13. Brewer, pp. 173, 166.

14. *Werke*, Sec. 1, I, liii.

15. "Jean Paul. Ein Stundenbuch für seine Verehrer," *Blätter für die Kunst*, in *Deutsche Dichtung*, eds. Stefan George und Karl Wolfskehl, (Berlin, 1923, 3rd ed.), p. 7.

16. *Werke*, Sec. 1, II, xxxvii.

17. Kommerell, p. 160.

18. Miller I, 29.

19. *Werke*, Sec. 1, II, x.

20. Miller I, 421.

21. *Werke*, Sec. 1, II, xxv.

22. Boeschenstein, p. 11.

23. *Ibid.*, p. 22.

24. Gerhart Baumann, *Jean Paul. Zum Verstehensprozess der Dichtung.* (Göttingen, 1967), p. 40. Hereafter cited as Baumann.

25. *Ibid.*, p. 24.

26. Miller I, 115.

27. *Ibid.*, pp. 221-24.

28. Gottfried von Strassburg, *Tristan und Isolde*, ed. Wolfgang Golther. (Berlin and Stuttgart, 1889), vv. 18019-18054.

29. Miller I, 305.

30. *Lodge*, p. 286.

31. Baumann, p. 13.

32. See Norbert Miller, *Der empfindsame Erzähler, Untersuchungen an Romananfängen des 18. Jahrhunderts.* (Munich, 1968), pp. 219, 304. Hereafter cited as Norbert Miller.

33. *Ibid.*, p. 303.

34. *Werke*, Sec. 1, II, xxxii.

35. Miller I, pp. 37, 52, 153, 154, 165.

36. *Ibid.*, p. 105.

37. *Ibid.*, p. 107.

38. Norbert Miller, pp. 217-18.

39. Miller I, 194.

40. Boeschenstein, p. 118.

41. Brewer, p. 174.

42. Baumann, pp. 15, 39, 41.

43. Boeschenstein, p. 126.

44. Walter Hoellerer, "Nachwort," in Miller I, 1312.

45. Brewer, *passim.*

46. *Lodge,* p. 364.

47. Miller I, 407.

48. *Lodge,* pp. 396-97.

49. Miller I, p. 1329.

50. Walter Harich, *Jean Paul.* (Leipzig, 1925), pp. 202, 216, 217, 247. Johannes Alt, *Jean Paul,* (Munich, 1925), pp. 83, 90, 93. Hereafter cited as Alt.

51. Miller I, 93.

52. Alt, p. 109.

53. Miller I, 240.

54. *Lodge,* pp. 380-82.

55. As quoted by Baumann, p. 41, translated by the author.

56. *Jean Pauls Werke,* II, 8.

57. *Werke,* Sec. 1, III, intr. Hans Bach, p. xxxvi.

58. Nerrlich, p. 230.

59. *Werke,* Sec. 1, III, xl.

60. *Jean Pauls Werke,* II, 1.

61. Kommerell, p. 83.

62. Baumann, p. 36.

63. *Werke,* Sec. 1, III, xxxv-xxxvii.

64. Harich, p. 306 f.

65. Jean Paul Friedrich Richter, *Hesperus,* tr. Charles T. Brooks, 2 vols. (Boston, 1865), II, 20-21. Hereafter cited as Brooks.

66. *Ibid.,* p. 315.

67. *Werke,* Sec. 1, III, xxiv-xxv.

68. Miller I, 1141.

69. Brooks, I, 490-491.

70. *Ibid.,* II, 177-78.

71. Norbert Miller, p. 312.

72. *Ibid.,* pp. 303, 323.

73. *Ibid.,* pp. 317-18.

74. Baumann, p. 37.

75. *Werke,* Sec. 3, I, 397.

Notes and References

Chapter Four

1. Emil Staiger, "Jean Paul: Titan," in *Meisterwerke deutscher Sprache*, 2nd ed. (Zurich, 1948), p. 56. Hereafter cited as Staiger.

2. See *Werke*, Sec. 1, XI, 250.

3. *Werke*, Sec. 1, VIII, lxxviii.

4. Christian Martin Wieland, unpublished "billet"; as quoted by Eduard Berend in *Werke*, Sec. 1, VIII, lxxviii.

5. See Wilhelm Scherer, *Geschichte der deutschen Literatur* (Berlin, 1908), p. 677.

6. Jean Paul, *Werke*, ed. Norbert Miller (Munich, 1961), III, pp. 900-901.

7. See Jean Paul, "Über die natürliche Magie der Einbildungskraft," as quoted by Staiger, p. 68.

8. Jean Paul Friedrich Richter, *The Campaner Thal and Other Writings*, tr. Juliette Bauer (Boston, 1864), p. 4.

9. Jean Paul Friedrich Richter, *Titan: a Romance*, 2 vols. tr. Charles T. Brooks (Boston, 1863), I, 161-62. Hereafter cited as *Titan*.

10. *Werke*, Sec. 1, VIII, pp. 205-206.

11. Staiger, p. 64.

12. *Ibid.*, p. 77.

13. *Werke*, Sec. 1, IX, 398, as quoted by Staiger, pp. 74-75.

14. *Titan*, II, 443; as quoted by Staiger, pp. 76-77.

15. *Werke*, Sec. 1, IX, 501; as quoted by Staiger, pp. 80-81.

16. *Ibid.*, XI, 267.

17. Anna Krüger, "Jean Pauls Humorlehre," *Hesperus: Blätter der Jean-Paul-Gesellschaft*, No. 13 (Bayreuth: Jean-Paul-Gesellschaft, 1957), p. 39.

18. Eduard Berend, "Anmerkungen," in *Werke*, Sec. 1, VIII, 536.

19. Kommerell, p. 207.

20. Eduard Berend, *Jean-Paul-Bibliographie*, 2nd. rev. and enl. ed., Johannes Krogoll (Stuttgart, 1963), nos. 1486, 2013, 2053, 2054, 2073, 2080, 2087, 2088, 2098, etc.

21. *Werke*, Sec. 1, VI, 176.

22. *Ibid.*

23. *Titan*, I, 2-3. All the following quotations from *Titan* are taken from this text.

24. *Werke*, Sec. 1, XI, 176.

25. *Ibid.*, p. 158.

26. *Werke*, Sec. 1, XI, 181.

27. *Ibid.*, p. 186.

28. *Ibid.*, p. 179.

29. Kommerell, pp. 30-31.

30. In *Zur Poetik des Romans,* ed. Volker Klotz (Darmstadt, 1965), pp. 32-47.

31. Sterne, as quoted by Victor Lange in *Zur Poetik des Romans,* p. 44.

32. *Ibid.,* p. 38.

33. *Werke,* Sec. 1, XI, 111-12.

34. Käte Hamburger, "Don Quijote und der epische Humor," in *Festgabe Berend,* eds. Hans Werner Seiffert and Bernhard Zeller (Weimar, 1959), p. 202.

35. Kommerell, p. 338.

36. *Werke,* Sec. 1, XI, 116.

37. Paul Böckmann, "Die humoristische Darstellungsweise Jean Pauls," in *Festgabe Berend,* p. 52.

Chapter Five

1. *Werke,* Sec. 1, VI, intr. Kurt Schreinert, pp. vi-vii. Hereafter cited as *Siebenkäs.*

2. *Ibid.,* p. xi.

3. *Ibid.,* p. xiii.

4. *Ibid.,* p. xix.

5. *Werke,* Sec. 1, XI, 197.

6. *Ibid.,* pp. 208-209.

7. Walter Rehm, *Jean Paul—Dostojewski: Eine Studie zur dichterischen Gestaltung des Unglaubens* (Göttingen, 1962).

8. As quoted by Rehm, p. 29.

9. *Ibid.,* p. 39.

10. *Ibid.,* p. 33.

11. See Wolfgang Kayser, "Wer erzählt den Roman?" in *Zur Poetik des Romans,* ed. Volker Klotz (Darmstadt, 1965), pp. 203-205.

12. The following examples are taken from *Siebenkäs,* p. 434. The English text is based on Jean Paul Friedrich Richter, *Flower, Fruit and Thorn Pieces: or the Married Life, Death, and Wedding of the Advocate of the Poor, Firmian Stanislaus Siebenkäs,* tr. Alexander Ewing (London, 1877), p. 456.

13. *Ibid.,* p. 560.

14. *Ibid.,* p. 563.

15. *Werke,* Sec. 1, XI, 234-35.

16. Edwin Muir, *The Structure of the Novel,* as quoted by Franz K. Stanzel in *Typische Formen des Romans,* 3rd ed. (Göttingen, 1967), p. 63.

17. *Ibid.,* p. 19.

18. *Ibid.,* p. 39.

19. *Ibid.,* p. 21.

Chapter Six

1. *Werke,* Sec. 1, X, lxii-lxiii.
2. *Ibid.,* pp. ix-lxiv.
3. "Jean Pauls vergnügtes Notenleben oder Notenmachen oder Notenlesen," in *Späte Studien* (Berne, 1964), pp. 7-96.
4. *Ibid.,* p. 16.
5. *Ibid.,* p. 22.
6. *Ibid.,* p. 30.
7. *Ibid.,* p. 36.
8. Jean Paul, *Walt and Vult; or The Twins,* 2 vols. tr. [Eliza B. Lee] (New York, 1846), I, 223. Hereafter cited as *Twins.*
9. *Twins,* I, 123-24.
10. *Werke,* Sec. 1, X, 493.
11. *Twins,* I, 182.
12. *Ibid.,* p. 247.
13. Elisabeth Endres, *Jean Paul: Die Struktur seiner Einbildungskraft* (Zürich, 1961).
14. *Werke,* Sec. 1, X, 333.
15. *Ibid.,* p. 332.
16. *Twins,* I, 196.
17. *Ibid.,* p. 279.
18. Kommerell, pp. 45-46.
19. *Werke,* Sec. 1, XI, 199.
20. *Ibid.,* p. 207.
21. *Ibid.,* p. 206.
22. *Ibid.,* p. 210.
23. *Ibid.,* p. 197.
24. *Twins,* I, 146. The following twenty-seven quotations are taken from the same text.
25. See Herman Meyer, "Jean Pauls *Flegeljahre,*" in *Der Deutsche Roman I,* ed. Benno von Wiese (Düsseldorf, 1965), p. 249.
26. J. W. Smeed, *Jean Paul's Dreams* (Oxford, 1966), pp. 18-31. Hereafter cited as Smeed.
27. Kommerell, pp. 183-84.
28. Smeed, p. 50.
29. *Ibid.,* p. 41.
30. *Ibid.,* pp. 96-97.
31. *Ibid.,* p. 98.
32. *Twins,* II, 308.
33. Smeed, p. 101.
34. *Twins,* II, 309.
35. Smeed, p. 104.

36. Ursula Gauhe, "Jean Pauls Traumdichtungen," Diss., Bonn, 1936.

37. Eva Baratta, "Sürrealistische Züge in Jean Pauls Werk," Diss., New York University, 1968.

38. *Ibid.*, p. 107.

39. *Ibid.*, p. 143.

40. *Ibid.*, pp. 128-29.

41. *Ibid.*, p. 146.

42. Peter Horst Neumann, *Jean Pauls "Flegeljahre"* (Göttingen, 1966), p. 103.

43. *Ibid.*, p. 113.

44. Louis Kampf, *On Modernism: the Prospects for Literature and Freedom* (Cambridge, 1967), p. 223.

Chapter Seven

1. *Jean Paul. Werke,* ed. Norbert Miller (Munich, 1965), vol. VI, "Nachwort" by Walter Hoellerer, p. 1366. Hereafter cited as Miller VI.

2. Harich, p. 804.

3. Jean Paul as quoted by Eduard Berend, *Werke,* Sec. 1, V, xxix.

4. Harich, p. 781 f.

5. *Werke,* Sec. 1, XV, xvii.

6. Kommerell, p. 388.

7. *Ibid.*, p. 390.

8. *Ibid.*, p. 371.

9. *Werke,* Sec. 1, XV, xvii.

10. Miller VI, 1367.

11. Kommerell, p. 384.

12. *Werke,* Sec. 1, V, liv.

Chapter Eight

1. Goethe's letter to Knebel in 1814, as quoted by Eduard Berend, in *Jean Pauls Werke,* V, 422.

2. Carl Reinhold, *Wörterbuch zu Jean Pauls Levana oder Erziehungslehre* (Leipzig, 1808).

3. Jean Paul, *Levana,* 3rd ed., tr. from the German (London, 1897), p. 83. All the following quotations from *Levana* are taken from this text.

4. Eduard Berend refers to Herder's *Ideas to a History of Mankind,* XV, 3; to Schiller's *On the Esthetic Education of Men,* Fourth

Notes and References

Letter; to Fichte's *Lectures on the Destiny of the Scholar*, all of them expressing similar ideas, as quoted in Jean Paul, *Werke*, ed. Norbert Miller (Munich, 1962) V, 1257. Hereafter cited as Miller V.

5. This was Jean Paul's answer to criticism in the *Hallesche Literaturzeitung* and in the *Zeitschrift für Pädagogik*. See Miller, V, 1257-58.

6. J. B. Basedow, *Des Elementarwerks erster bis vierter Band. . . .* (Dessau, 1774) as quoted by Miller, V, 1261.

7. Anton Luible, "Pestalozzi und Jean Paul," Diss. (Kempten, 1912), p. 4. Hereafter cited as Luible.

8. Miller, V, 1266.

9. Miller, V, 1275.

10. Luible, pp. 24 and 39.

11. Jean Paul, *Übungen im Denken*, as quoted by Luible, p. 35.

12. Wilhelm Münch, *Jean Paul, der Verfasser der "Levana,"* (Berlin, 1907); Benedikt Picht, "Die Verwirklichung der Ideen der Levana in der Pädagogik Rudolf Steiners," *Erziehungskunst*, XXVII (1963), 74-91.

Epilogue

1. See Edward V. Brewer, *The New England Interest in Jean Paul Friedrich Richter* (Berkeley and Los Angeles, University of California Press, 1943), pp. 18, 20.

2. *Ibid.*, p. 3.

3. Thomas Carlyle, "Jean Paul Friedrich Richter," *The Book-Worm*, II, 13 (July, 1885), p. 11.

4. Jean Paul, posthumous maxim, as quoted by Eduard Berend in his *Jean-Paul-Bibliographie* (Berlin, 1925), p. 40.

Selected Bibliography

A complete bibliography on Jean Paul can be found in Eduard Berend, *Jean-Paul-Bibliographie,* revised and enlarged by Johannes Krogoll (Stuttgart: Ernst Klett Verlag, 1963). It contains 2904 titles, a table of contents, and three indices, which facilitate its use.

Fuhrmann, Eike. "Jean-Paul-Bibliography, 1963-1965," *JJPG* I, (1966), 163-79, constitutes a supplement.

PRIMARY SOURCES

EDITIONS

1. Complete Works:

The historical-critical edition by Eduard Berend as cited below is recommended as basis for research. E.B. presented his plans for this edition to the Prussian Academy in 1927; they appeared under the title, *Prolegomena zur historisch-kritischen Gesamtausgabe von Jean Pauls Werken.* (Abhandlungen der Preussischen Akademie der Wissenschaften, 1927, Phil.-Hist. Klasse, I.) Berlin: de Gruyter & Co., 1927.

Jean Pauls Sämtliche Werke. Historisch-kritische Ausgabe, eds. Preussische Akademie der Wissenschaften in Verbindung mit der Akademie zur Erforschung und zur Pflege des Deutschtums [Deutsche Akademie], 1934 ff.; Deutsche Akademie der Wissenschaften zu Berlin, 1952 ff.; und Jean-Paul-Gesellschaft. Weimar: Böhlau, 1927 ff.; Berlin: Akademie-Verlag, 1952 ff.

This edition has three sections:

I. The works published during J.P.'s lifetime, checked against the manuscripts and J.P.'s own lists of errata. Each volume contains an introduction which lists the sources, models, the genesis, and the reception of the work. Footnotes explain unfamiliar references. The variants to these critical texts were to be printed separately; but only volume I, 19, edited by Paul Stapf, was published, 1944; it covers "Greenland Lawsuits," "Selection from the Devil's Papers," and "The Invisible Lodge" and it is of little scholarly value.

II. The literary remains. Only five volumes out of thirty-seven have been published. They contain J.P.'s notes from his "repositorium," preliminary studies, biographical notes, and finished but unpublished works.

III. The correspondence, complete with variants, notes, and indices of correspondents. 8 vols. Vol. IX contains addenda, corrections, supplements, and an index of names with valuable explanations.

2. Selected Works:

Jean Pauls Werke, ed. Eduard Berend. 5 vols. Berlin: Propyläen-Verlag, 1923.

Jean Paul. *Werke,* ed. Norbert Miller (Vol. II ed. Gustav Lohmann). 6 vols. Munich: Hanser, 1959-1963. Among the fifteen collections of J.P.'s work published during the last hundred years, these two are the best ones.

3. Single Works:

There are 140 reprints of single works, eleven of them published by Reclam. We mention only

Jean Paul's *Schulmeisterlein Wutz.* (Anglica Germanica V.) Ed. Eva J. Engel.'s Gravenhage: Mouton & Co., 1962. Highly recommendable for the American reader who has a reading knowledge of German. German text with English introduction, annotations, and appendices.

4. Anthologies:

[George, Stefan]. "Jean Paul. Ein Stundenbuch für seine Verehrer," *Blätter für die Kunst.* Berlin, 1900. See also Stefan George under Secondary. Sources.

[Kemp, Friedhelm, Norbert Miller and Georg Philipp, eds.]. *Jean Paul. Werk, Leben, Wirkung.* Munich: Piper, 1963. A popular, worthwhile introduction. Selections of various texts, also judgments on J.P. by famous contemporaries and by posterity.

5. Translations:

Only available in larger libraries. Forty-eight published before 1850, nineteen before 1900 and three before 1950, showing the growth and decline of J.P.'s fame in the English-speaking countries. Berend's bibliography lists 67 titles under the heading of English and

American translations. Below, selected translations are listed according to the first publication date of J.P.'s works; their German title is given in brackets.

The Invisible Lodge. [*Die unsichtbare Loge, 1793.*] Tr. Charles T. Brooks (Leisure Hour Series 154.) New York: Holt, 1883.

"Life of the Cheerful Schoolmaster Maria Wutz." ["Leben des vergnügten Schulmeisterleins Maria Wuz in Auenthal," *Die unsichtbare Loge,* 1793.] Tr. John D. Grayson. *Nineteenth Century German Tales,* ed. Angel Flores. (Doubleday Anchor Books, No. 184). New York: Doubleday, 1959, pp. 1-37. The only work of J.P. still commercially available in English.

"Wutz" is the German favorite. First English translation: *Maria Wuz and Lorenz Stark: or English prints of two German originals.* Tr. F. and R. Storr. London: Longman, Green & Co., 1881, 5-45.

"Extract from the nineteenth dog's post day, of the second volume of Jean Paul's *Hesperus.*" [Hesperus, oder 45 Hundsposttage, 1795.] Tr. J—. *The German Museum,* II, London, 1800, 525-30. This is the first translation of J.P. by the same unknown author who mentioned J.P. earliest in England; see under Secondary Sources.

Life of Quintus Fixlein, extracted from fifteen Letterboxes. [*Leben des Quintus Fixlein, aus fünfzehn Zettelkästen gezogen. . . . ,* 1796.] Tr. Thomas Carlyle.
Jean Paul Friedrich Richter, Edinburgh, London, 1827; see under Secondary Sources. Carlyle added his translation of *Fixlein* to his book review on J.P.'s Biography, 1830; see under Secondary Sources. Carlyle's translation can also be found in *The German Classics of the nineteenth and twentieth Centuries.* Masterpieces of German Literature translated into English. Ed. Kuno Francke. New York: The German Publication Society, 1913, IV.

"The Death of an Angel." "The Moon: a tale of the Imagination." ["Der Tod eines Engels." "Der Mond, eine phantasierende Geschichte." *Leben des Quintus Fixlein . . . ,* 1796.] Tr. Richard Holcroft. *Tales from the German.* London: Longman, 1826. Also in Holcroft, *Tales of Humour and Romance.* London, New York, 1829. Carlyle had excluded these two introductory stories to *Fixlein.* "The Death of an Angel." Tr. S-. C-. T-. *Knickerbocker,* XVII. New York, 1841, 495. Also in Henry Morley, *The dream of the Lilybell, tales and poems;* with translation of the "Hymns to night" from the German of Novalis and Jean Paul's "Death of an Angel." London: Sherwood, Gilbert and Piper, 1845. Also in Alfred Baskerville, *Beauties of German Literature*. Selections from various authors. London: Burns, 1846. "The Moon." Tr. John Oxenford. *Tales from the German, comprising specimens from the most celebrated authors*. London, New York: Chapman and Hall, 1844, 261-68. Also in *Godey's Lady's Book and Magazine*, XLVI. Philadelphia, 1853, 497.

"The New Year's Night of an Unhappy Man." [Die Neujahrsnacht eines verdorbnen Jünglings." *Jean Pauls Briefe*, 1799. First publication 1796.] Tr. Hermann Bokum. *Translations in poetry and prose from celebrated German writers*. Boston: Munroe, 1836. This text, which was translated into English seven times, is hardly known in Germany. Also in *Knickerbocker*, xx. New York, 1842, 475. See also Henry Reeve, "Translations from Jean Paul," *Nineteenth Century*, III. Philadelphia, 1849, 211. "The New Year's Night of an Unhappy Man." Put into verse by James Clarence Mangan, *Dublin University Magazine* (1835), 400. Reprints in *Anthologia Germanica*. German anthology; a series of translations from the most popular of the German poets, I. Dublin, 1845, 194-96 and Mangan, *Poems*. Dublin, 1886, 132.

Flower, Fruit and Thorn Pieces: or the Married Life, Death, and Wedding of the Advocate of the Poor, Firmian Stanislaus Siebenkäs. [Blumen- Frucht- und Dornenstücke; oder Ehestand, Tod und Hochzeit des Armenadvokaten F. St. Siebenkäs . . . , 1796/ 97.] Tr. Edward Henry Noel. London: William Smith; Boston: Munroe, 1845. Boston: Ticknor and Fields, 1863; Leipzig: Tauchnitz (Collection of German Authors IX, xx), 1871. Noel was the first one to translate a novel as a whole.

Flower, Fruit, and Thorn Pieces; or, the wedded life, death and marriage of Firmian Stanislaus Siebenkaes, parished advocate in the burgh of Kuhschnappel. (A genuine thorn piece.) Tr. Alexander Ewing. (Bohn's Standard Library.) London: George Bell and Sons, 1877 and 1886. London: Little, Brown and Scribner, 1888.

"The Speech of Christ." [Rede des todten Christus vom Weltgebäude herab, dass kein Gott sey," *Siebenkäs*, Erstes Blumenstück.] Tr. Thomas Carlyle, review of "Wahrheit aus Jean Paul's Leben" [Biography of Jean Paul], in *The Foreign Review and Continental Miscellany*, V, ix. London, 1830, 1-52. Reprint "The Atheist's Dream," *Western Messenger*, II. Louisville, 1836, 243.

See also A. Kenney, "Speech of Christ," in *The Death of an Angel* . . . , London: Black and Armstrong; Dresden and Leipsic: Chr. Arnold, 1839, "The Vision of a Godless World," *National Magazine,* III. New York, 1853, 262.

Henry Nevinson, "Lament of the dead Shakespeare among the dead congregation in Church because there is no God." ["Des todten Shakespeare Klage unter todten Zuschauern in der Kirche, dass kein Gott sei." J.P.'s original version.] *A sketch of Herder and his time.* London, 1884, 448-50.

Paul C.A. Dachsel, *Poetical version of Richter's "Speech of Christ" and miscellaneous poems.* Sheboygan, Wis.: Dachsel, 1898.

The Campaner Thal: or, discourses on the immortality of the soul. [*Das Kampaner Thal oder über die Unsterblichkeit der Seele* . . . , 1797.] Tr. Juliette Gowa. London: Gilpin, 1848. Second rev. ed. London: Gilpin, 1857; Boston, 1864. Review by C. T. Brooks, *North American Review,* XCIV. Boston, 1864, 587-92. Brooks is the expert in the field of J.P. translations. See also Jean Paul Richter. *The Campaner Thal,* and other writings. Boston, 1864.

Titan, A romance. [*Titan,* 1800-1803.] Tr. Charles T. Brooks. Boston: Ticknor and Fields; London: Trübner, 1862, I-II. This is an almost flawless translation of the novel that J.P. considered his masterpiece.

For a passage from the novel, the description of Rome, also translated by Brooks, see "Johann Paul Friedrich Richter," *Prose Writers of Germany,* ed. Frederic Henry Hedge. Philadelphia: Carey and Hart, 1848. Reprint in *The German Classics of the nineteenth and twentieth Centuries.* Masterpieces of German Literature translated into English. Ed. Kuno Francke. New York: The German Publication Society, 1913. IV.

Brooks's earliest publication is a versification of passages from *Titan* in *Songs and Ballads; translated from Uhland, Körner, Bürger, and other German lyric poets.* Boston: J. Munroe, 1842.

Walt and Vult, or The Twins. [*Flegeljahre,* 1804-1805.] Tr. Eliza B. Lee. Boston: Munroe; New York: Wiley, 1846, I-II. E.B. Lee is the author of *Life of Jean Paul;* see under Secondary Sources.

"Summer time in Germany." [*Sommers-Zeit, Flegeljahre,* ch. 19.] Tr. H.W. Longfellow. This is the best translation of ch. 19.

Knickerbocker, XXII. New York, 1843, 87. Reprinted as "A Summer Night" in *International Monthly Magazine*, I. New York, 1850, 38.

"The happy Life of a Parish Priest in Sweden." ["Das Glück eines schwedischen Pfarrers," *Flegeljahre*, Teutonizans]. *The London Magazine*, IV, xxiv. London, 1821, 615-20. Reprints in De Quincey, *Works*. Edinburgh, 1863, XIII, and "Confessions of an English Opium-eater," London, 1867. See De Quincey under Secondary Sources.

"Van der Kabel's last will and testament." [*Flegeljahre*, ch. 1.] Tr. Hans Müller-Casenov, *The Humour of Germany*. London, New York, 1909.

See also "The Opening of the Will," tr. Frances H. King in *The German Classics of the nineteenth and twentieth Centuries*, ed. Kuno Francke, as above.

Levana; or The Doctrine of Education. [*Levana oder Erziehungslehre*, 1807.] Tr. A-. H-. London: Longman, 1848, XX. Further eds. Boston: Ticknor and Fields, 1863, XXI, and 1866. Revised ed. "under the eye of the original translator," preceded by a short biography of the author and his autobiography, a fragment. (Bohn's Standard Library.) London: George Bell and sons, 1876, 1884, 1897.

Levana appears six times on the list of translations in E.B.'s bibliography.

"*Army-Chaplain Schmelzle's Journey to Flaetz; with a running Commentary of Notes*. [*Des Feldpredigers Schmelzle Reise nach Flätz mit fortgehenden Noten . . .*, 1809.] Tr. Thomas Carlyle in *Jean Paul Friedrich Richter*. Edinburgh, London, 1827; see under Secondary Sources.

SECONDARY SOURCES

1. In German

ALT, JOHANNES. *Jean Paul*. Munich: Beck, 1925. Not profound but still the best introduction to J.P.; combines biography, discussion of works, relations to the time, and evaluation. See Fritz Martini, "Jean-Paul-Forschung und Jean-Paul-Literatur. Ein Bericht," *Deutsche Vierteljahrsschrift für Literaturwissenschaft und Geistesgeschichte*, XIV (1936), 305-23.

BAUMGARTNER, BERNHARD. "Sprachstruktur in Jean Pauls Roman *Flegeljahre*." Unpublished dissertation, Erlangen, 1959. Defines J.P.'s style as mannerism, as opposed to classicism. J.P. does not want to imitate nature but to create a world of his own, as manifested in his metaphorical style.

BEREND, EDUARD. *Jean Paul und die Schweiz*. (Die Schweiz im deutschen Geistesleben, 89.) Frauenfeld/Leipzig: Huber & Co., 1943. Contains J.P.'s correspondence with Lavater, Joh. v. Müller, Mummenthaler, A. Heune, and others, some of it published for the first time. See also Eduard Berend, "Jean Paul und die Schweiz," *Neue Zürcher Zeitung*, November 15, 1925.

————, ed. *Jean Pauls Persönlichkeit in Berichten der Zeitgenossen* [J.P.'s personality in reports of his contemporaries]. Berlin: Akademie-Verlag; Weimar: Böhlau, 1956. (First published Munich and Leipzig: Georg Müller, 1913.) This is a supplement to E.B.'s historical-critical edition of J.P.'s complete works.

BÖCKMANN, PAUL. "Die humoristische Darstellungsweise Jean Pauls," *Festgabe Berend*, eds. H.W. Seiffert and B. Zeller (Weimar: Böhlau, 1959), pp. 38-53.

DILTHEY, WILHELM. "Jean Paul," *Von deutscher Dichtung und Musik*. Leipzig, Berlin: Teubner, 1933, pp. 428-63.

ENDRES, ELISABETH. *Jean Paul: Die Struktur seiner Einbildungskraft*, Zürich: Atlantis-Verlag, 1961.

GEORGE, STEFAN. "Lobrede auf Jean Paul," *Blätter für die Kunst*, März 1896, pp. 59-62. For reprints see *Blätter für die Kunst*, ————. "Jean Paul," *Der Teppich des Lebens und die Lieder von Traum und Tod*. Berlin: Georg Bondi, 1900, 1919. George influenced an increasing number of Germans to turn to J.P. as one of their greatest authors who cannot be labeled a Romanticist or a representative of Biedermeier, but is a genius in his own right.

GOETHE, JOHANN WOLFGANG VON. "Vergleichung," *West-Oestlicher Divan*. Stuttgart: Cotta, 1819. Goethe, who had originally rejected J.P., whose metaphorical style seemed far-fetched to him, gained a new understanding by comparing J.P. to the poets of the East.

HARICH, WALTER. *Jean Paul*. Leipzig: Haessel, 1925. 860 pp. H. sees J.P. slightly distorted by playing Goethe and Schiller off against him.

Selected Bibliography

HARICH, WOLFGANG. *Jean Pauls Kritik des philosophischen Egoismus.* Frankfurt am Main: Suhrkamp, 1968.

HOFMANNSTHAL, HUGO VON. "Blick auf Jean Paul. 1763-1913," originally in *Neue Freie Presse* (Vienna) March 23, 1913. Reprinted in *Prosa 3.* Frankfurt M., 1952. H., like Stefan George, has an ear for the musicality of J.P.'s language and for the enchantment emanating from his idylls: but he admits that we live in a different world.

KOMMERELL, MAX. *Jean Paul.* Frankfurt M.: Klostermann, 1923; 1939 (supplemented with preface and index); 1957. K. upholds J.P.'s greatness; he praises him as the boldest renewer of German prose style, and places J.P. the humorist next to Shakespeare, Cervantes, Swift, and Sterne.

KRUGER, ANNA. "Jean Pauls Humorlehre," *Hesperus,* XIII (March, 1957), 35-39.

————. *Der humoristische Roman mit gegensätzlich verschränkter Bauform. Jean Paul, Wilhelm Raabe, Kurt Kluge.* Limburg/Lahn: Vereinsdruckerei, 1952.

————. "Die humoristische Darstellungsform im *Siebenkäs.*" *Hesperus* V (März, 1953), 21-24. Based on the above diss.

————. "Wuz und Quintus Fixlein. Eine vergleichende Betrachtung," *Hesperus,* XXI (März, 1961), 27-34.

LANGE, VIKTOR. "Erzählformen im Roman des 18. Jahrhunderts," in *Zur Poetik des Romans,* ed. Volker Klotz (Darmstadt: Wissenschaftliche Buchgesellschaft, 1965).

LOERKE, OSKAR. "Das unbekannteste Genie: Ein Versuch über Jean Paul," *Die neue Rundschau,* XXXV (September 1924), 915-39. Reprinted with slight changes in *Zeitgenossen aus vielen Zeiten* (Berlin, 1925).

LUIBLE, ANTON. *Pestalozzi und Jean Paul.* Diss., Kempten: J. Kösel, 1912.

MEYER, H[ERMAN]. "Der humoristische Sonderling bei Jean Paul," *Neophilologus,* XXV (1940), 252-64.

MINDER, ROBERT. "Jean Paul in Frankreich," *Festgabe Berend,* 1959. Reprint in *Dichter in der Gesellschaft: Erfahrungen mit deutscher und französischer Literatur.* Frankfurt M.: Insel-Verlag, 1966.

————. "Jean Paul oder die Verlassenheit des Genius," in *Dichter in der Gesellschaft*. . . . Both essays were originally written in French, then translated into German by the author, who recognizes the influence of political, sociological, and economic factors on the poet, as well as that of spiritual, religious, and esthetic movements.

MULLER, JOSEPH. *Jean Paul und seine Bedeutung für die Gegenwart.* Sec. rev. ed. Leipzig: Meiner, 1923. All aspects of Jean Paul's life are discussed; literary criticism is slighted.

MUNCH, WILHELM. *Jean Paul, der Verfasser der Levana.* Berlin: Reuther und Reichard, 1907.

MUSCHG, WALTER. "Der Zauberer Jean Paul," *Studien zur tragischen Literaturgeschichte.* Berne, Munich: Francke, 1965. Like Baumgärtner, Muschg calls J.P. "the founder of romantic mannerism" and, in addition, "the father of surrealism" and "The Magician."

NERRLICH, PAUL. *Jean Paul. Sein Leben und seine Werke.* Berlin: Weidmann, 1889. N.'s monograph deals with philosophy, literary criticism, and esthetics and uses Fr. Th. Vischer, Hegel's successor, as a criterion in order to examine J.P.'s work from the viewpoint of religion.

PICHT, BENEDIKT. "Die Verwirklichung der Ideen der Levana in der Pädagogik Rudolf Steiners," in *Erziehungskunst,* XXVII (1963), 74-91.

RASCH, WOLFDIETRICH. *Die Erzählweise Jean Pauls. Metaphernspiele und dissonante Strukturen.* Munich: Hanser, 1961. Rasch defines J.P.'s style as interruptive. This unepic style is not caused by eccentricity but rather by necessity: J.P. needed freedom for the creation of his world.

REHM, WALTHER. "Experimentum suae medietatis. Eine Studie zur dichterischen Gestaltung des Unglaubens bei Jean Paul und Dostojewski," *Jahrbuch des Freien Deutschen Hochstifts* (Frankfurt M., 1940), pp. 237-336. Reprinted in R.'s *Experimentum medietatis, Studien zur Geistes- und Literaturgeschichte des 19. Jahrhunderts* (Munich, 1947), pp. 7-95. Revised version in *Jean Paul—Dostojewski. Eine Studie zur dichterischen Gestaltung des Unglaubens* (Kleine Vandenhoeck-Reihe 149/150). Göttingen, Zürich: Vandenhoeck, 1962.

————. "Jean Pauls vergnügtes Notenleben oder Notenmachen und Notenlesen. Eduard Berend post festum gewidmet," *Jahrbuch der Deutschen Schillergesellschaft,* III (Stuttgart, 1959), 244-337. Rehm points out that in J.P.'s work the footnotes are a structural element of the epic texture.

REINHOLD, CARL [PSEUD. ZACH. LEHMANN]. *Wörterbuch zu Jean Paul's "Levana oder Erziehungslehre."* Leipzig: Eurich, 1809.

SCHACHT, FRANK E. "Jean Paul im Lichte der englischen und amerikanischen Kritik des 19. Jahrhunderts," in *Festgabe Berend,* 1959.

————. ed. "Die weissen und die blauen Blätter. Henry Wadsworth Longfellows Aufzeichnungen und Vorlesungen über Jean Pauls Leben und Werke," bearbeitet und übersetzt. *Hesperus* XX (Oktober, 1960), 32-36. Longfellow planned to write a biography of J.P. but used his notes for lectures; see also Longfellow's *Hyperion.*

SCHLEGEL, FRIEDRICH. "[Fragment über Friedrich Richter]," *Athenäum,* I, ii (Berlin, 1798), p. 131.

SCHNEIDER, GEORG (TEXT) UND RICHARD SATTELMAIR (BILD). *Jean Paul: Leben, Werk und Deutung.* Würzburg: Echter-Verlag; Zürich: NZN-Verlag, 1963. Contains 72 pages of pictures and 48 pages of text; a best seller in 1963.

SPAZIER, RICHARD OTTO. *Jean Paul Friedrich Richter. Ein biographischer Commentar zu dessen Werken.* 5 vols. Leipzig: Brüggemann & Wigand, 1833. Spazier was J.P.'s nephew. He was twenty-two years old when his uncle died. He spent the last weeks with him, helping him to prepare the complete edition of his works.

STAEL, HOLSTEIN, MME LA BARONNE DE. *De l'Allemagne.* Paris: H. Nicolle, 1810. Part II, ch. 28, contains a passage on J.P. with an incomplete translation of the "Speech of the dead Christ," mainly written by Ch. Villers. The first edition was confiscated. Reprints: London, 1813; Berlin, 1814, etc.

STAIGER, EMIL. "Jean Paul: *Titan.* Vorstudien zu einer Auslegung," *Meisterwerke deutscher Sprache aus dem neunzehnten Jahrhundert.* Zurich, Berlin: Atlantis-Verlag, 1943. My discussion of J.P.'s style as developed in *Titan* is based on this essay.

WOLFSKEHL, KARL. "Dämon und Philister. [Jean Paul Friedrich Richter.]," *Der Querschnitt,* VII (1927), 265-70. Reprint: Wolfskehl, *Bild und Gesetz* (Berlin, Zurich, 1930), pp. 38-45.

2. In English

The earliest mention of J.P. in England is by the unknown author of the "Extract from the nineteenth dog's post day." [Notiz über Jean Paul Richter.] *The German Museum,* I (London, 1800), p. 69. J.P. is criticized for his poor taste but compared to Shakespeare and Sterne.

BREWER, EDWARD V. *The New England Interest in J. P. F. Richter.* Berkeley and Los Angeles: University of California Press, 1943.

[CARLYLE, THOMAS]. *Jean Paul Friedrich Richter.* (German Romance: specimens of its chief authors; with biographical and critical notices. By the translator of *Wilhelm Meister,* and author of the life of Schiller, III.) Edinburgh, London, 1827. Carlyle was the best-known admirer of J.P. in England. See also *Army-Chaplain Schmelzle's Journey to Flaetz* under Translations.

[————], Reviewer. "Wahrheit aus Jean Paul's Leben" [Biography of Jean Paul]. 3 vols., Breslau, 1826, 1827, 1828. *The Foreign Review and continental miscellany,* V (January, 1830), 1-52. This review of J.P.'s Biography contains translations from excerpts of *Vorschule, Fixlein, Hesperus,* and "die Rede des toten Christus."

DE QUINCEY, THOMAS. "John Paul Frederick Richter," *The London Magazine,* IV (December, 1821), 600-612. Written in the form of a letter dated Grasmere, October 18, 1821, under the name of Grasmeriensis Teutonizans. Following this letter, De Q. published a translation of the third chapter of the "Twin Brothers," see under Translations.

[LEE, ELIZA BUCKMINSTER]. *Life of Jean Paul Frederic Richter.* Compiled from various sources. Together with his Autobiography. Translated from the German. 2 vols. Boston: Little and Brown, 1842. One copy, with handwritten dedication of Carlyle to Varnhagen, still available at Deutsche Staatsbibliothek, Berlin. Editions with new title page: London: Chapman, 1845, 1849, 1851, 1864 (Chapman's Catholic Series). Annex of Vol. II contains selections of *Kampaner Thal.*

[LONGFELLOW, HENRY WADSWORTH]. *Hyperion, a Romance.* By the author of "Outre-Mer." New York: S. Colman, 1839. The protagonist is informed by an inhabitant of Bayreuth, who knew J.P., about the latter's life.

Selected Bibliography

RECKLING-ALTENHEIM, MARGARETE. *Jean Paul's Reception in the 19th and 20th Centuries.* An Abridgment of thesis, New York University, 1938.

SMEED, JOHN WILLIAM. *The Problem of Dualism in the Works of Jean Paul.* Thesis accepted for higher degrees. University of Wales, 1955.

————. "Surrealistic Features in Jean Paul's Art," *German Life and Letters,* XIX (Oct. 1965).

————. *Jean Paul's "Dreams".* London: Oxford University Press, 1966.

Index

(The works of Richter are listed under his name)

Aristotle, 70
Augustine, St., 87

Bach, Hans, 52
Baratta, Eva, 124-25
Basedow, Johann B., 131, 135
Baudelaire, Charles, 87
Baumann, Gerhart, 43
Benn, Gottfried, 46
Berend, Eduard, 17, 31, 39, 98, 104, 121
Berlepsch, Emilie von, 24
Boeschenstein, Bernard, 39, 46
Borowski, Ludwig E., 32
Böckmann, Paul, 82
Böhme, Jacob, 123
Brentano, Clemens, 39
Brewer, Edward V., 46
Brooks, Charles Timothy, 150
Büchner, Georg, 87

Carlyle, Thomas, 150
Cervantes, Miguel de, 78, 100; *Don Quixote*, 61, 127-29
Cicero, 20, 70

Dante Alighieri: *Divine Comedy*, 32
der Hagen, Friedrich von: *Nibelungenlied*, 127
Dostoevsky, Feodor, 87
d'Urfé, Honoré: *L'Astrée*, 46

Eichendorff, Joseph von, 112
Eschenbach, Wolfram von, 75-77; *Parzival*, 55, 77

Feuchtersleben, Karoline von, 24
Fichte, Johann Gottlieb, 26, 62, 64
Fielding, Henry, 76, 78, 93
Fischart, Johannes, 75-76
Flaubert, Gustave, 87
Follen, Karl, 150
Forster, E. M., 51

Gauhe, Ursula, 124-25
George, Stefan, 41, 59
Goerres, Joseph, 127
Goethe, Johann Wolfgang von, 18, 23, 38, 45, 73, 87, 126, 131; *Dichtung und Wahrheit*, 130; *Elective Affinities*, 83; *Faust*, 61; *Iphiginie*, 33; *Tasso*, 33; *Werther*, 20, 50, 110; *Wilhelm Meister*, 55, 93
Grass, Günther, 75-76; *The Tin Drum*, 39
Grimm, Jacob: "Hans im Glück," 98
Grimmelshausen, Jakob Christoffel von: *Simplizissimus*, 83
Gundolf, Friedrich, 113

Hebbel, Friedrich, 29-30
Hedge, Frederic Henry, 150
Heine, Heinrich, 87
Hemsterhuis, Franz, 144
Herder, Johann Gottfried von, 23, 28, 51, 144
Herold, Karoline, 22
Hildburghausen, Duke of, 24
Hoffmann, E. T. A., 26, 39

Hofmannsthal, Hugo von, 46
Horace, 20

Jacobi, Fritz, 144
Jacobsen, J. P., 87

Kalb, Charlotte von, 23, 24
Kalidasa: *Sakontala*, 51
Kampf, Louis, 125
Kant, Immanuel, 32
Kayser, Wolfgang, 88
Keller, Gottfried: *Green Henry*, 55, 87
Kierkegaard, Sören, 87
Klopstock, Friedrich Gottlieb, 67, 88
Kommerell, Max, 18, 29, 65-66, 73, 76, 122

Lange, Victor: "Erzählformen im Roman des 18. Jahrhunderts," 76, 78
Lavater, Johann Kaspar, 23
Leibniz, Baron Gottfried Wilhelm von, 101
Lessing, Gotthold Ephraim, 66-67
Lichtenberg, Georg Christoph, 20
Longfellow, William Wordsworth, 150; "Summertime in Germany" (tr. of Richter), 105
Louis XVI, 53
Luible, Anton, 149

Matzdorff, Karl, 38
Mayer, Johann Siegfried Wilhelm, 24
Meyer, Hermann, 120
Meyern: *Dya-Na-Sore*, 50-51
Miller, Johann Martin: *Siegwart*, 20

Miller, Norbert, 44-45
Milton, John: *Paradise Lost*, 32
Montaigne, Michel de, 134
Moritz, Karl Philipp, 50; *Anton Reiser*, 38
Mozart, Wolfgang Amadeus: *Magic Flute*, 59, 145
Musil, Robert, 46, 50
Musset, Alfred de, 87
Münch, Wilhelm, 149

Neumann, Peter Horst, 125
Novalis, 39, 100

Oerthel, Lorenz Adolf von, 19-20
Osmund, Emanuel, 25, 27, 127
Otto, Amoene, 26
Otto, Christian, 25, 26, 27, 39, 42, 53, 54, 83
Ovid: *Ars Amatoria*, 145

Pascal, Blaise, 87
Paulus, Heinrich, 26
Paulus, Sophie, 26
Pestalozzi, Johann Heinrich, 131, 147, 149; *Buch der Mütter*, 140; *Wie Gertrud ihre Kinder lehrt*, 140
Plato, 144
Pope, Alexander, 20

Rabelais, François, 93
Rehm, Walter: "Jean Pauls vergnügtes Notenleben oder Notenmachen oder Notenlesen," 87, 100-102
Richardson, Samuel, 76, 78, 93
Richter, Emma (daughter), 25, 112, 131, 134
Richter, Jean Paul Friedrich: birth, 17; childhood, 18-19; at Gymnasium in Hof, 19-20; at University of Leipzig, 20;

90174

uses pen name J.P.F. Hasus, 21 and JEAN PAUL, 23; private tutor in Schwarzenbach, 21; vision and conversion, 22-23, 27; marriage, 25, 99; receives honorary doctorate from Heidelberg University, 26; blindness, 27; death, 27

Works:
Abelard and Heloïse, 19-20
Against Super-Christianity, 27
Autobiography (unfinished), 17, 80
Booklet of Freedom, 27
Clavis Fichtiana, 79
Comet, The, 126-30
Comic Appendix to Titan, 44, 52, 59, 64, 79, 99
Conjectural Biography, 25
Dr. Katzenberger's Trip to a Spa, 31
Flegeljahre, see The Twins
Flower, Fruit and Thorn Pieces: or the Married Life, Death, and Wedding of the Advocate of the Poor, Firmian Stanislaus Siebenkäs in the Imperial Market-Town of Kuhschnappel, see Siebenkäs
Freudel's Lamentations, 31
Greenland Lawsuits or Satirical Sketches, 20-21
Hesperus, 23, 38, 49-54, 58, 77, 80, 83, 97, 101-2, 126, 128, 129
Introduction to Esthetics, 25, 28-29, 63, 68, 72, 85, 87, 93, 99, 110, 119
Invisible Lodge, The, 23, 30, 38-49, 50, 52-53, 58, 80, 83, 97, 126, 128, 129, 150

Levana; or the Doctrine of Education, 25, 131-49
Life of Fibel, 29, 31-37, 80
Life of the Cheerful Schoolmaster Maria Wutz, 23, 28-31, 35, 38, 43, 55, 98
Logbook of the Balloonist Giannozzo, 64-65, 79, 97
My Own Funeral, 83
Parson in Jubilee, The, 80
Quintus Fixlein, 29, 31, 80, 83
Selections from the Devil's papers, 27
Selina, 27
Sermon on Peace, 27
Siebenkäs, 23, 25 ,44, 55, 64, 83-95, 98, 101, 110, 126, 144
Titan, 23, 38, 44, 52, 55-82, 85, 87, 96, 97, 98, 121, 126, 128, 129
Trip of the Military Chaplain to Flätz, 31, 101
Twilights for Germany, 27
Twin-Brothers, The, see The Twins
Twins, The, 25, 31, 44, 62, 64, 80, 96-125, 126
Valley of Campan, The, or Discourse on the Immortality of the Soul, 27

Richter, Johann Christian (father), 18, 20
Richter, Karoline Mayer (wife), 24-26, 137
Richter, Max (son), 25, 27, 112, 131, 138
Richter, Odilie (daughter), 25, 26, 112, 131
Richter, Sophie Rosine (mother), 17, 21, 23
Robespierre, Maximilien de, 53
Rollwenzel, Mrs. Dorothea, 26

Rousseau, Jean Jacques, 23, 28-29, 39, 131, 134-35, 148; *Confessions*, 139; *Emile*, 131, 137

Savigny, Friedrich Karl von, 26
Schelling, Friedrich Wilhelm von, 26
Scherer, Wilhelm, 59
Schiller, Friedrich von, 19, 23, 28, 32; *Naive and Sentimental Poetry*, 28
Schlabrendorf, Countess, 24
Schlegel, Friedrich, 39, 107; *On the Language and Wisdom of the Indians*, 51
Schlegel, August Wilhelm, 39
Scudéry, George and Magdeleine: *Cleli*, 46; *The Grand Cyrus*, 45-46
Seneca, 20
Shakespeare, William, 93
Smeed, J. W., 123
Spangenberg, Beata von, 19-20
Spazier, Richard Otto, 35
Staiger, Emil, 55, 59, 61, 62

Stanzel, Franz K., 94
Sterne, Laurence, 46, 54, 76; *Tristram Shandy*, 44-45, 120
Strassburg, Gottfried von, 41, 43
Strich, Fritz, 39
Swift, Jonathan, 20, 63, 81; *Gulliver's Travels*, 29

Thieriot, Paul Emil, 137
Tieck, Ludwig, 31, 39, 127

Valéry, Paul, 46
Vischer, Theodor: *Auch Einer*, 31
Voltaire, François Marie Arouet de, 20
Voss, Heinrich, Jr., 26, 27

Wagner, Richard, 41
Wieland, Christoph Martin, 23, 93; *Agathon*, 55
Woolf, Virginia: "The Narrow Bridge of Art," 49

Young, Edward, 20